RUNNING IS LIFE

Transcending the Crisis of Modernity

Bruce Fleming

University Press of America,® Inc.
Lanham · Boulder · New York · Toronto · Plymouth, UK

Copyright © 2010 by
Bruce Fleming
4501 Forbes Boulevard
Suite 200
Lanham, Maryland 20706
UPA Acquisitions Department (301) 459-3366

Estover Road
Plymouth PL6 7PY
United Kingdom

Library of Congress Control Number: 2010925374
ISBN: 978-0-7618-5175-2 (paperback : alk. paper)
eISBN: 978-0-7618-5176-9

Introduction

It's unclear what percentage of real communication in the twenty-first century takes place in books, but most cultural commentators agree that this percentage is rapidly diminishing, victim of more immediate and accessible, not to mention short-winded means of getting our thoughts out to others. Meanwhile book publishing seems to exemplify the basic economic definition of inflation, which is "too much money chasing too few goods." In today's publishing world, virtually all are agreed that, with the exception of the blockbusters, too many books are chasing too few readers. It's not even the readers chasing the books, but the other way around, as if the food on our table came off the plate and into our faces, begging to be eaten: and then more and more! We'd all flee.

The fascination with celebrities that seems so dominant a feature of today's world characterizes the world of publishing as well: the few books that are read and discussed are those that "everyone" is reading and discussing; best-sellers kill the mid-list, popularity begets popularity. You want to be reading what your friends are reading, which probably means something discussed on television, if you read anything at all. And, as any editor will tell you, this rules out most males, who tend to bond over sports rather than books: readers today are overwhelmingly female, so books published tend to be what women want. Book publication is, after all, a business, and nowadays all of it is at least highly commercial; commercial publishers are completely commercial.

But aside from these "gotta have it" titles, book publishing is caught in a vicious circle: book readers are fewer, and titles are more numerous. An economic hurdle for book publication is the old model of print runs, which requires money up front for printing and rental on the cartons of books, not to mention a dependency relationship to bookstores that get a 40% discount off cover price and can return all unsold copies with no penalty. Print-on-demand (POD) technology that eliminates the print runs, the storage, and the bookstore, has made possible the publication of practically anything and everything. So coinciding with a radical drop in readers is an explosion in the number of titles available. The company Bowker, which puts out *Books in Print*, calculates the number of new titles in the U.S. alone during 2008 at more than half a million titles, with a 3% diminution of print-run books and an explosion of print-on-demand titles, more than 100% with respect to 2007.[1]

But that means for every book of which any note at all is taken, there are tens of thousands more, of which no notice whatever is taken. And this is to a degree causal. In a world that can send "The Three Tenors" on tour to sports arenas, it's something of a shock to realize that the world has many more tenors that might bring the same enjoyment to music fans—except if the basis of that enjoyment is the exclusive thrill of hearing "the" three tenors, which it apparently largely is. How else to explain the rock-star appeal of the ageing and increasingly forced-sounding Luciano Pavarotti when he wowed the crowds in football stadiums? The people who would go to see Pavarotti in a football arena regardless of how he sings are not the people who would swell the rout for a chamber music concert another time.

Anything where somebody else has to advance money up front is in fast retreat; anything where the investment is minimal (and usually paid by the author or artist) is in radical expansion. So book publication is both shriveling and expanding exponentially at the same time. The result is that publication now means something different than it used to: now it's a more private thing, like putting on amateur theatricals or making house chamber music. Those are concerts too, and suddenly count as shows. Only the number of people who come to them are minimal, and their quality is usually quite low.

Book publication is a victim of its own success: anybody can do it, simply by paying money to an electronic or POD service such as iUniverse or Xlibris; the result, though rarely reaching an audience greater than the family members of the author. To peruse online publications about POD publishers, many small-town "authors" are taken in by come-on lines promising "availability" in bookstores (which means that bookstores can, in theory, order them, though many decline to order non-returnable POD books, which are printed by a machine only when there's a direct order for them—that's what "print on demand" means) and illusions about the meaning of "publication." It's a sad world, that of what amounts to printing services for personal ruminations, one fueled by the money that people are willing to pay to be "published."

We can therefore argue about whether this is the winter or summer of book publication, depending on whether we want to emphasize the fact that anybody can publish (or "publish") a book or instead the fact that very few titles of whatever sort every get more than a few readers. What's clear at any rate is that the meaning of "publication" is different than what many people think: publication doesn't mean anybody wants it. Publishing a book nowadays in some venues is like putting on a show on a street corner for the cars whizzing past to glance at, and listing yourself as a "performing artist" on your resume.

So all in all the number of ideas transmitted in books may be small, both because (outside of the best-sellers) few people read the books and few books are read. They exist, somewhere, on an electronic list, but they might as well not.

Some authors, evoking clichés of the unappreciated Romantic artist, take bitter pride in the fact that they have no audience. That must mean that they're destined for posthumous fame! How many people read Kant when he was alive, for instance, curling up with a glass of sherry and the *Kritik der reinen Vernunft* on a cold Prussian night? And look at his reputation now! But this is a false converse, the belief that merely to be ignored in one's time guarantees posthumous immortality merely because we can cite a few cases where subsequently famous authors were in fact ignored during their lifetimes. It's a common error, and probably some consolation for people who slave so hard for so little reward. Gertrude Stein, for one instance, seems to have believed that being overlooked meant she was a great writer; this makes reading *The Autobiography of Alice B. Toklas* somewhat painful—albeit odd, as she did in fact achieve celebrity, through just such works as this apologia.

The bottom line is, writing a book doesn't seem to have much point.

Still, authors persist. Why?

It's a platitude of contemporary cultural criticism that technology from e-mail to Twitter has reduced the size of our communal unit of attention. The same was said for the medium of television before it became so ubiquitous as to have faded into the background (in 2010 I spent two days in the hospital where the television played 24/7 to empty rooms, and to full ones too: even the gas pumps where I fill my car kick into a television program for a minute or two while that gas is pumping, as if afraid to leave us idle for that long). And it may be true that our collective attention span is short: students in colleges (I've taught at one for more than two decades, albeit a rather strange one, the U.S. Naval Academy) seem impatient with ideas so nuanced as to require time for their development, as all contemporary media seem impatient with ideas that are more complex than the sound bite, and appear not to understand the necessity of providing justification for their positions: if they believe it, they seem to feel, they're good to go.

So readers are unlikely. Then the question becomes, What does writing do for the writer?

Writing a book provides a refuge from the world of short attention spans, a calmer, more ordered world where ideas give way to related ideas, where responses to the world can be offered one by one, in proper order, in a way they rarely can be in the more chaotic real world. The world of a book, whether written or read, is like the sound-proof acoustically crisp world of a concert hall on which so much money and expertise is expended (many people agree that after multiple make-overs, engineers may finally have gotten New York's Avery Fisher [Philharmonic] Hall something close to right). A concert hall is artificial too: it shuts out the world of the street so we can concentrate on just this sequence of sounds imagined by the composer and brought to reality by the conductor and musicians, just these nuances of dynamics and interpretation. This is true even if the music (or for some, "music") played is that of John Cage, consisting of playing several radios set at different stations simultaneously: if this controlled cacophony had to compete with the uncontrolled cacophony of the street noise from Amsterdam Avenue outside Avery Fisher Hall, we wouldn't get the point of this either.

So a book is an artificial world. But it's no more artificial than the dark black boxes of movie theaters, the carefully lit boxes of art galleries (the architect Renzo Piano is much praised for his filtered lighting in museums such as Houston's Menil Collection), or the "don't tread on me" white space that surrounds poems on the page. Or, for that matter, the specific world of a rock concert, or the stadium of people gathered to pay homage to "The Three Tenors." The thing about such artificial worlds is, you can't force people to enter them. That's their beauty, and their point: people choose to enter the isolation chambers of such sub-worlds as books—they can't do it on the fly. In order to enter them you need to be not too hungry, not too preoccupied, not too worried, not too fearful. Try entering Avery Fisher Hall to concentrate on Beethoven just after you've lost your job. You may be able to make the jump, but I doubt it. Most of life *can* be experienced on the fly. Not concerts, not artworks, and not books, either to make them yourself or to experience what others have made.

We live in an age and under circumstances that may seem relentlessly antithetical to the book. Circumstances may be antithetical to the success or reception of specific books, indeed of the overwhelming majority of books available to ever-diminishing numbers of readers. Yet neither the age nor circumstances can be inimical to the Idea of a book, that of an enclosed world like a walled-in garden. Here, we can concentrate.

And so, another book.

Bruce Fleming
Annapolis, Maryland
2 January 2010

1
The Problem with Modernity

The opening of Ludwig Wittgenstein's *Tractatus Logico-Philosophicus* reads, in German:. *Die Welt ist alles, Was der Fall ist.* Turned around and translated into idiomatic English, this gives the point of departure for my hymn to the sublime and sweaty act of running for its own sake, simultaneously self-affirming and self-annihilating: Everything that is, is the world. If it's here, it's here, and it's part of everything that is. Facts are facts, things are things, and all of that is life.

You'd think this is common sense: the world is everything that's so—as Wittgenstein's ideas read in the order he wrote them. Why is this worth writing down? Nowadays we say, to end the conversation about something we know isn't going to change, "It is what it is." This means: accept it. And indeed, to say that the world is what it is, as Wittgenstein is apparently saying, is meant (as the end of the *Tractatus* makes clear) to get people to shut up and move on. That's the way it is. Now move on.

That it is something of a let-down is clear: we'd like the world to be not just what it is, but, somehow, something else. But what? Perhaps, what it could be, what we imagine it to be, what we strive to have it be while knowing it isn't and perhaps can never be. The disappointment of the modern world is precisely this: to realize that each person has equal access to the world. Look around you: there it is. That's what there is. And that's *all* there is. Not very exciting, is it? This is the problem with modernity.

To say that the world is what it is, is deflating. Somehow it doesn't seem enough; people seem to go on wanting more than what's here. Robert Browning's much-quoted line from his poem "Andrea del Sarto" acknowledges this desire while throwing cold water on it: "a man's reach should exceed his grasp, Or what's a heaven for?" We'll only get something beyond our grasp when we're dead. In the meantime there is, gulp, the world. Live with it; it is what it is.

Most people in this modern age don't deny that this is so; we just don't *want* it to be so. We're like the character in the Borscht-belt joke about the person who wouldn't want to be a member of any club that would have him as a member. If the world is ours, it isn't alluring; it doesn't pull us on. How could it? It's here already.

Sure, we can enjoy it, as we're allowed to do in the modern age with nobody trying to take it away from us. The U.S. Declaration of Independence guarantees us "the pursuit of happiness." But what if we don't know what happiness is except by looking at what other people think happiness is? We can work to acquire more material things. But what do we do when our children take them for granted? What's the purpose of life? The individual has access to all there is; and that's precisely the problem.

Being modern in the West means precisely to accept, albeit sometimes and to some degree unwillingly, that there isn't much that can transcend the individual. Though there are naysayers to the weary Western assertion of the primacy of the individual, they are, at least for the moment, largely in retreat. In the West, it seems, we may long for something more exciting than each person left alone to pursue his or her own ideal of happiness—namely, having everyone pursue the same ideal. But usually we back off, realizing that having the pursuit be general means running over the rights of dissenters or the less enthusiastic— and the realization that constraint means force, and force means a police state or war, or both.

These desires occasionally have resurgences, to be sure, as the moral fervor of the U.S. under President George W. Bush can be argued to have been a resurgence of the notion of national or cultural purpose that transcends individuals. And outside the West there is a much greater tolerance for such myths of collective purpose, perhaps most specifically the religious. But such attempts usually end badly, whether within the West or outside of it, since collective redemption, to the extent that it is (temporarily) achieved, is only achieved at others' expense—and some day the bill always comes due as these others get their revenge. Collective boredom, it seems, is the price we pay for peace. Or if not boredom, then an acceptance of the limitation of life. Surely this explains the fact that the last two centuries and counting, as a result, are dotted with the disastrous nineteenth- and twentieth-century attempts of Communism, fascism, and religious fervor to move society toward an apotheosis that transcends the fragmented desires of the individuals of which it is made— instances where societies did not back off from longing for something larger, stronger, and more powerful than the sum total of individual desires to give a purpose to life.

We pay lip service to the sanctity of individual conscience, but may always be prey to wanting more. Religion in the modern West has largely been relegated—at least in theory—to the limited, if for that reason secure, niche of personal belief: we have the right to believe what we believe, only not the right to force others to believe it too. Somehow that seems to fly in the face of the notion of transcendence: if this belief transcends, it transcends the individual, which means that everyone else ought to believe it too. Why not just go for it?

Fascism too may be a lurking temptation for the modern mind, that occasionally prove too tantalizing to resist. And the thing about fascism is that it can only be put into practice on a grand scale: it's grand opera, not chamber music. As for example the form of secular transcendence attempted through the Hitlerian belief in German hegemony. If this had been the vision of a single man he'd have ended in a madhouse. Secular transcendence can only succeed on a grand scale, or fail just as absolutely. Given that this was the vision of a society, the world was nearly destroyed. You can't dream a dream of national destiny without involving the whole nation any more than you can play a Mahler symphony on the harmonica—not without being ridiculous, anyway. Or funny. (The puppeteer Basil Twist set Berlioz's "Symphony Fantastique" to the twitches of abstract cloth shapes in a "stage" several feet across; part of the charm of Twist's response was the disproportion between what we heard— grand evocations of ballrooms, scaffolds, and a witches' ball—and the tattered ridiculousness of what we saw: the Romantics would not have approved.)[2]

So the big dreams are so seductive because they're big. And that's also why they're so destructive when they fail, as inevitably they do.

Are we all then to stick strictly to our own little beliefs, our own little pleasures, our slippers and our contentment before the fire, our politeness and our getting along with the neighbors, our respect for others and our unwillingness to force others to do what they don't want to do? How dreary it all seems, if full-lit and without shadows, how banal. It seems the victory of all the smug Philistines the English aesthetics railed against, the victory of Baudelaire's hated *bourgeoisie*, the Belgian businessmen who went strolling on Sunday in the park, followed by wife and children. Compared to the horrors of Bosnia or Rwanda, this seems pretty good. But compared to, well, adventure, it's horror. If you've lived the horror, or are capable of learning from history, you're probably pretty happy with the Sunday stroll in the park. But if you grew up with this and don't read, you probably pine for stronger meat.

For the dreamer in us—and which of us is capable of being satisfied with the world as it is?—this all seems horrible. Dostoyevsky's *Notes from Underground* is an assertion of the thought, perhaps an earlier pre-echo of Freud's, that people aren't most intrinsically rational creatures bent on their own preservation, but instead comical, quizzical, unpredictable and even as a result self-destructive creatures. This desire to transcend the banality of the quotidian, of the what-belongs-to-us (if it's ours it can't be any good), is what causes problems for modernity now as in Dostoevsky's nineteenth century. People don't, apparently, want to be predictable, scientific, and modern: they're not satisfied. Or maybe they're just devilish. Vast theologies pre-dating the problem of the modern are founded on the perception that people, puzzlingly, don't always do, or even seem to want to do, what's right.

This either/or is the problem of the modern. In terms of that classic modern novel, Flaubert's *Madame Bovary*, the choices are between, on one hand, marital respectability that involves crushing boredom with a man who understands nothing, and on the other, illicit affairs with unworthy men and death by suicide. Yet putting the choices as only these extremes is the sign of Flaubert's modernity, and the fact that there is no option in the middle what I am calling the crisis of the modern. I propose in this book to transcend the crisis of the modern.

Let's agree that a world without any redemption beyond what the individual can achieve for him- or herself is rather discouraging. How can the individual transcend, if not at others' expense and collectively? The answer is, by running. In running we go beyond ourselves—and if we do it right, nobody else cares. Unlike organized sports that require gear and arenas, jogging only needs a pair of shoes that most people in the U.S. today wear to go shopping, and the wide open spaces of the outdoors.

It's true that in running we don't achieve transcendence. But we do transcend the crisis: we learn that it's not true that our only two choices are Madame Bovary's extremes. We learn that transcendence isn't something achieved, it's something engaged in: transcendence is an action—individual action. We needn't dream of collective transfiguration: that at any rate is only short-lived, and not a long-term solution to what otherwise seems the flatness of the individual's world. We can't transcend life—that's impossible. But we do transcend the belief that it can be transcended. The problem of modernity is precisely the belief that life needs to be, and can be, moved beyond: in running we transcend this belief, not life itself.

The despairing modern asks: is there nothing between boredom on one hand and destruction on the other? *Running is Life* suggests there is: it lies in active participation in the everyday, setting goals for ourselves that we alone can achieve, and then setting new ones. It suggests that we have to reconcile ourselves to the fact that lurid dreams of collective meaning are just that: dreams. And then we set out to achieve what in fact we can achieve, in action, the act of running.

Life is good, but we have to make it that way; we are who we are, but we have to discover who that person is. This gives meaning to each person's life that is an alternative to the fascist dreams of collective transcendence and transfiguration, the swelling music that always ends in death and destruction, as well as to the satisfied pettiness of the person thrilled to be an obedient consumer of things he or she has to be taught to desire. There's an alternative to both: running is life.

2
Running is Life

Every runner has transcendent memories of running on that perfect day when the spring is just poking through, or the fall beginning to shiver a yellow leaf or two from the trees, when the air is neither too hot nor too cold, the sun shimmering with the breath of the new-born day or beginning to grow cloudy with oncoming night, the ground as much rising to meet feet as feet pounding the earth, the air entering the body as if the body were lunging forward to enclose the air. If you know the feeling, you don't need words to describe it. If you don't know the feeling, words won't do it justice.

This moment of perfect union of self and world, movement and the silent blur, is the justification not only for running, but also talking, or writing, about running. Thus it must come at the beginning of any consideration of running. Yet writing about running that stopped with this moment of rarely attainable bliss wouldn't be very long. The moment of bliss, this "what it's all about," is the ineffable, the thing that goes beyond expression, what transcends words.

A book about running can therefore only take us up to this moment—the way Wittgenstein thought his *Tractatus* could only take us up to the things that cannot be said, the words (could we only say them) that would underlie all words: what he called "the mystical," what can't be expressed.[3] Running is to words *about* running as Wittgenstein's inexpressible "mystical" is to language in general. Falling silent is only the end of words, not of anything else.

To be alive is to move. As soon as we're born we begin to move, and death comes only when we are still. Within seconds of birth we cry and then we suck; later we clench our fists around adult fingers and learn to roll over, then to sit up, then to crawl, and then to walk, at every stop channeling the urge to move into motion forward. Motion always wins over stasis: every morning we start moving again, and have re-arranged a dozen times in the course of the night. At the end of a session of thinking or writing, during which at least our fingers and heads moved, we get up and stretch, like a cat waking up from a nap. We're out of the shallows into the open sea.

The bare minimum of normal everyday movement, for adult life (with the exception of people with disabilities) is walking. When we run, we take the urge to move expressed in basic locomotion; then we turn this into something we can control. We run because we want to, at least in the sense of running I'm talking about here—not, say, trying to catch a bus. When we run "just because," we can stop at any time, and for this reason are aware of the action of running as something we control: it takes over our bodies and our selves, but it does so at our express invitation. Running is a way of simultaneously acknowledging the transcendent as something beyond the everyday and integrating it into the world—through action.

Philosophers have disagreed regarding the relationship of the transcendent to the world of the here and now: we want to believe in a realm beyond our own, usually held to give meaning to our quotidian lives. But the problem is precisely that to be transcendent, it has to be beyond our lives—perhaps even beyond our perception. Plato was clear that the transcendent existed, though in another realm—which a select few could access through contemplation, whatever that means (we still don't know after millennia). Wittgenstein seemed to agree, at least partially: he held that transcendent meaning might well exist, but if it did, the fact that it was transcendent meant we'd never get at it, at least not in words. Some of Wittgenstein's disciples concluded from this that any sentence that tried to speak of transcendent meaning (as in statements, say, about value, or about The Good or The Beautiful) must simply be nonsense. But clearly Wittgenstein had a soft spot for such nonsense. His point wasn't that the transcendent didn't exist, only that if we could achieve it, it wouldn't be transcendent.

Thus his conclusion that the *Tractatus* was like a ladder that, once having climbed, we could push away.[4] His words rendered themselves useless, and as a result, it seems that writing, or reading, his words, implied a paradox. How can we talk ourselves into silence?

Had Wittgenstein been a runner, the fact that he had to bring us to the point where we wouldn't need him—the point where we shouldn't have needed him to begin with, this point between immanence and transcendence—would not have seemed a contradiction. He would simply have finished writing, and gone for a run. In running, all words stop: we go beyond words into action for its own sake.

We solve Wittgenstein's paradox through running. Running shows us that Wittgenstein was right, only he didn't go far enough. Transcendence isn't, in fact, achieved in words; instead it's achieved in action. Running isn't in the realm of Plato's Ideas—but then nothing we can actually get at could be. It's as transcendent as the mundane can get: nothing else bridges the gap, given that we're stuck on the side of the mundane, looking outwards—not the reverse.

Urn

Failing to realize that transcendence can be achieved (insofar as it can be achieved) through our action was the weakness of the poet John Keats as well, a notably contemplative sort rather than an active one. (Think how the course of Western philosophy might have changed if the Romantic poets had been athletic, or had Wittgenstein been encouraged to take up jogging.) Keats noted in his "Ode on a Grecian Urn" that if we could ever achieve a state beyond reality, we'd cease to be human. What he failed to see is that what transcends reality isn't a state, it's an action. And it's also part of reality: transcendence itself isn't transcendent—if it were, as Wittgenstein points out, it wouldn't be attainable.

What's carved on Keats's urn, among other things, is a young man in the pink of physical health (he's so beautiful he might even be a god), reaching out for a woman he's chasing on a summer's day. Keats' point is that it's the reaching out that's the perfect moment, the striving for the goal rather than the attaining of the goal that's the height of human existence. When we get the goal, assuming we do, we don't want it any more, because we have it. And like as not we'll get tired of it, or the very fact of having it, or of not striving, and set off after another goal. According to Keats, only something frozen and artificial like the urn stops the endless cycle typical in life whose stages are first setting a goal and working towards it, then (possibly) achieving it, then being disappointed because it's something we possess (and hence no longer a goal), then having to set a new goal we haven't yet achieved. The repetitive nature of it all comes from the fact that in life, a goal achieved is no longer a goal. Thus in life we can never stop the cycle; in this sense the urn is better than we are, always beyond our grasp.

This is Keats's conclusion, yet it is too negative. Running for its own sake, where the goal is the action itself, transcends this endless cycle of achievement, disappointment, and setting new goals. Transcendence isn't a place, it isn't a state, and it certainly isn't an object. It's found in action for its own sake, most clearly in the action of running.

Tube

This means real, not metaphoric, running: pounding pavement or grass, sweating, our arms swinging rhythmically, sucking air, feeling ourselves on the cusp of over-reaching ourselves. Many early twentieth century thinkers invoked metaphors of motion to capture human existence, yet did so without meaning sweat and blood-pumping running.

Heidegger, in his *Being and Time*, wrote of the *Geworfenheit* of existence, its "thrownness": the fact that we're projected into time as a pre-condition of our lives.[5] Virginia Woolf, one of the Modernists, wrote movingly of life as like being "blown through the Tube at 50 miles per hour . . . with one's hair flying back like the tail or a race-horse."[6] It's not clear that either Heidegger or Virginia Woolf ever set out to run—really run, with their knees up, swinging their arms, their hearts pounding—as an end in itself. Probably their running, if any there was limited to those times when they were late. This isn't running, it's the trotting in street clothes we do in emergencies, something we stop as soon as it's no longer necessary. Thus the vision of the motion of life of both the phenomenologists and the Modernists seems a willy-nilly, passive thing. We're thrown, we're blown. Whether we like it or not, this is going to happen.

When I was an undergraduate philosophy major, one of my professors, at that point still under the influence of the philosopher Gilbert Ryle, spoke of Descartes'[7] "schoolboy howler" (a "howler" is British slang for a really ridiculous mistake) of presupposing the "I". *Cogito ergo sum*, said Descartes: I think, therefore, I am. But if there is no "I" to think or be, what is left? Silly old Descartes, so blatantly begging the question. Descartes, once seen as so fundamental to Western philosophy, by then (my professor sniffed) shown to be useless by people like Ryle, or Heidegger, with their insistence that (according to Ryle) there was no soul, no "ghost in the machine," and that (according to Heidegger) the first thing we had to do was rid ourselves of the influence of Socrates, that old believer in clear distinctions and rationality.[8] Now, it seemed, we knew that things were essentially flux. Things don't stand still. Existence, said Sartre, following Husserl, precedes essence: we *are* before we are *any specific thing*.

These philosophers meant to bury previous philosophy, and then read its epitaph. They wanted to have the last word. Yet philosophy begets philosophy— every attempt to kill it only adds to it. The history of philosophy is like a pile of books I made one day with volumes I was pulling out of boxes that had lain long dormant in my mother's attic. The first handful of books, from the cardboard of the box rotten and falling to pieces under my fingers from decades in the heat of summer and the cold of winter, and dusty as well, was already somewhat haphazard, small books on top of large and not well centered. As a result, in order to balance these, the second handful of books was set off-center on the first; the next off-center too, in the opposite direction, the whole fairly stable only because books by now stuck out in all directions, each over-balance of the pile in one direction engendering and balancing the over-direction in the next.

Philosophy is always a response to what preceded it, always out to correct an imbalance with what, it turns out, is an equal and opposite imbalance, that in turn will be unbalanced in another direction, engendering the need for yet a further imbalance. Philosophy teeters between Plato, pointing upwards to the Heavens or the realm of Ideas in Raphael's celebrated "School of Athens," and Aristotle, standing beside him in the same painting, his hand held out flat over the ground—not the "series of footnotes to Plato" that Alfred North Whitehead imagined.[9] We can look up, or down, or in the middle: and then all over again.

All of this vast never-ending line of add-ons dwarfs the individual and any collection of individuals or intellectual movements, brief flare-ups that soon die down. Yet the whole cycle, the whole wobbly pile, is encapsulated in, transcended, and given flesh by running, something any individual can do over and over. Running goes beyond philosophy. We express the immanent, and gesture towards the transcendent. That's as good as it gets.

Free will

Running puts an end to many philosophical quarrels. For instance, running silences this question: do I have free will or do I not?

I might note a desire to reach out and pick up the coffee cup by the side of my computer. (Usually I don't note the desire, I just pick up the coffee: this fact is already significant, as it indicates that desire has to separate from action, it isn't separated intrinsically, and so doesn't always need to be justified.) Or do I merely desire the coffee, the reaching out being the means to achieving this goal rather than the goal itself? Whatever the nature of the desire, I would say I am the author of that desire. But—so the objection goes—I may be wrong that "I" "desire" anything. Perhaps this situation is the expression of a biological need for caffeine, an effect of smell on olfactory glands, the result of habit or societal convention, or the will of God. What is this desire, this want? But if we can ask, What is this "want"?, we should perhaps more fundamentally ask, "What is the 'I' that wants?" Perhaps the self isn't a distinct entity at all. Do we, we suddenly wonder, even have a soul? Are we more than mere biology? Discussions like this, that fill countless journals and books, are just what running makes unnecessary.

Running transcends other questions too, like these: What makes me me? What is the nature of the self? Descartes' enterprise, in his *Meditations*, was to systematically doubt that his senses were giving him true evidence: he thought he saw other people, but did he? Perhaps they were only mechanical dolls. He is able to find his way back to certainty and "common sense" by reasoning that though everything he thought might be wrong—the doubt proved justified—he couldn't doubt the fact of thinking. His conclusion was that this fact, the fact that he thought anything at all (even if he was wrong in the content of what he thought), was the bedrock of his certainty: the fact that because he thought, he knew he existed. *Cogito, ergo sum.*

Philosophy R Not Us

But what's so puzzling about philosophy is the assumption that we need words at all. The most fundamental questions—for example: Do we have a soul? Do we have free will?—are the most fundamental precisely because we can give any answer and carry on as before: no answer, whatever it is, changes anything. It doesn't ultimately matter whether we decide that we have a soul, or whether we insist that, say, science has shown this to be a myth. Let's say we go with the second. If science shows us we don't have one, then we never had it: it's not like the magic trick of the disappearing rabbit where one moment we see the rabbit, or have a soul, the next moment we don't. We have to conclude that what we took to be signs of the soul weren't that at all. It's not the facts that change, only our interpretation of them.

In the same way, the shadow we thought was that of Chain-saw Charlie can turn out to be the cat, magnified by an angle of the lamp; the twinges we took to be those of X can turn out to have been Y instead. Nobody says we didn't feel the twinges, didn't see the shadow. It was there, and it meant something, only not what we thought it did. When the person we're dating smiles at us we want to think it means one thing: perhaps it doesn't, it means something else. Time may be the only way we'll ever know. But we weren't wrong that we saw the things we saw. The only thing we're arguing about is the label we put on them.

The strangeness of philosophical debate is that people get attached in turn to the labels they attach to the phenomena: yes we have a soul, no we don't. Yes we have free will, no we don't. Neither label changes the state of things, so what does either matter unless we've gotten attached to the labels? People in the everyday world, to be sure, get attached to some labels, such as those expressed by race and sexuality; philosophers get attached to others. Typically philosophers can see that labels in the world outside have become their own end (black/white, gay/straight)—and almost invariably denounce this focus on the secondary. They are not so good at seeing how secondary their own labels are in turn.

Say it's decided we don't have free will. Can't I still reach for my coffee? I was doing so a moment ago, when I thought I had free will but apparently didn't. To say that some questions are more fundamental than others—questions we can answer, like "Is there a fly on the wall?"—doesn't actually mean they're more vital, or more important. Just that they'll always be with us: we can see that we don't need to answer them from the fact that nobody ever has. It seems, after all, that we can live our whole life on shifting sands of never having an answer. Or maybe the sands aren't shifting: maybe that's as stable as it gets. If life seemed stable before, but is actually shifting, maybe that's what we mean by "stable"—for "shifting" to apply, we have to see something different. Maybe objective is the same as subjective. Fine. So what do we call the distinction between these two now? Why not stick with "objective" and "subjective"?

Most of the atoms in the void simply shoot past each other: there's so much empty space. A rare few collide. Philosophy, the specialized study of asking questions, finds all the places where the atoms collide and strings them together saying: Here, this is philosophy. They want us to believe that the world revolves around questions like, Do we have free will or not? This implies a contrary force, a collision: one side says we do, the other that we don't. But there are a million other atoms that simply don't engage with the statement "Human beings have free will." Eating a peanut butter sandwich, taking out the recycling bottles, comforting a child, picking up the trash on the local creek—none of these engage with this statement, nor do the objects themselves, the peanut butter, the bottles, the creek, or the trash. Nor even all words: the statement that "it's a nice day today" or the salutation "How are things going?" don't intersect even tangentially with Big Metaphysical Questions.

You have to look long and hard to find something that is close enough to the statement that "Human beings have free will" that it even threatens to collide with it. Philosophy first limits its attention to asteroids rather than the space junk, and then, further, to the incalculably smaller group of cases where an asteroid collides with something. These collisions are presented as representative of the world, because they are all that philosophy considers, and then presents the consideration as a model of the world.

Yet there are far more misses than collisions; and further out than misses, we get nothing at all, no interaction at all. So when a philosopher devotes a whole class period, or a whole semester-long class, to the question, "Do human beings have free will?" s/he is searching far and wide for the tiny number of bits of the universe relevant to this question. The whole infinity of things won't change to any perceptible amount whatever we decide: there will still be peanut butter sandwiches, whether or not we have free will. And we can eat them, or not.

Eating a peanut-butter sandwich, like taking out the garbage or reading a novel, offers an alternative to philosophy too. All these things are what we can do in life to show us that there is a good deal that transcends words. Yet what they do primarily is assuage hunger pangs, or keep us sanitary, or amused. They transcend philosophy only as a side effect. Of all the things we could do in the world to go the next step beyond philosophy, running for running's sake (rather than to catch a bus) is the most direct because it doesn't do much else than this, at least not while we're doing it. It acknowledges others by entering into the stage sets of their actions, engaging in an action that's a speeded-up version of the basic force of life. It's both part of life and beyond it, a meaningful action whose primary fact is to be what it is.

Autumn
One fall morning, I go for a run at home. It's unnaturally warm, and a bit rainy. I leave the t-shirt the corner to pick up on the way back. I love the feel of air against my skin; better yet is rain. It's a mystery to me why some people won't run in the rain: they're going to get sweaty anyway, the rain feels good, and besides you're going to throw the clothes in the washer at the end, or wring them out and hang them out to dry. And the fact that it was overcast kept the sun out of my eyes.

When I run from home, I follow an out-and-back course, with a turn-around. It's two different courses, the two directions. Leaving, I'm conscious of the sense of having accomplished something when I'm up the first hill; coming back, I run backwards down the hill, it isn't anything at all, and it seems almost the end. "Up and Back" is one of the standard patterns of running. In addition, there is the "Great Loop," and there is "Running the Track," the repeated loop. Each is a sort of metaphysical statement translated into action: the line, the circle, and the spiral, three forms that life can take.

It was almost the end of fall: the rain had taken down many of the leaves, which were strewn across the wet ground. The road, and most of the grass, were covered with them. Some of the road, and thus my running route, which follows the asphalt in a rough parallel, is across open pasture: here the grass was green; too green, in fact, with the moisture and this too-warm weekend. The grass was dotted with red and brown leaves. In some parts of the run, the colors were almost earth-tone fluorescent: a whole field of soybeans had been left to dry to a kind of glistening brown, with the sun trying to come through the clouds in bits and snatches falling on the too-green clover on the other side of the road, the almost purple of the Japanese maple leaves strewn across them. It was like entering a world re-done by Post-Impressionists, moving through a Gauguin painting. And under the canopy of another hill, where the trees meet over the road, all was sun-struck brown: the remaining leaves, the now naked branches around them, the glistening burnt umber leaves on the ground.

Because of this change in the colors—the fall version of the spring alteration, the blossoming into fragile green—the whole run was caught between familiarity and the new. The objects were the same as always, and the hills, the trees in the same place. But the colors were different, the ground obscured by leaves almost not there, the trees suddenly denuded, different. In running through this suddenly so-active world, I'd be conscious of a few steps or the squishy ground for a moment, then be lost in the colors, in the slippage between what I expected and what I saw—and then, abruptly, realize I was a half mile further on in the route. Running isn't putting one foot in front of the other, it's dissolving into the world for longer or shorter periods of time and then coming to one's self and to the ground, and then once again becoming part of the world: here, part of the world of the shifting colors, of the cows, of the sky trying once again to lighten and then become overcast. It's about the change of focus between sharp definition on objects and the blurring the division between the self and the objective world.

This was a familiar world rendered new by season variation. The world we run in can be new for other reasons too: we've never seen it. Running up the incline of the Mount Whitney Portal Road (Mount Whitney, at 14, 496 ft., is the tallest mountain in the continental United States) from Lone Pine, California, I leave the neat but run-down houses of the town behind. There is a small horse farm on the outskirts of town; the road runs up its center and then rejoins the road. The ascent is continuous and relentless. I run past the entrance to the Alabama Hills, the strange arrangement of blobby rocks at the base of the mountains where countless Westerns have been shot, including the Lone Ranger series. A bit further on is the Los Angeles aquifer, a concrete-lined ditch that directs the mountain snow melt to the distant city of Los Angeles. It starts on the other side of the road and channels the water under the blacktop I'm running on.

I stop to watch it carrying the water away: I am breathing heavily because of the ascent, standing on top of the concrete ribbon that has dessicated this whole valley. Nobody is here but me; for this brief moment it's mine, no matter who has been here before and who may come later. Around the curve is a hill, on the right, where someone—or many someones, working together—has spelled out "Mt. Whitney" in huge stone letters: I decide that I will make rounding that hill my goal. Now I am plodding, putting one foot in front of the other, feeling the air huff and puff from my lungs. Finally I am at my turn-around point and start down, running backwards most of the way, like watching a movie on re-wind. In all this time, only one car has passed me, and the sun is only now up.

We can also run in cities to discover them. What the *flâneur* –the walker through the streets of Paris—was to the 19th century, the urban jogger is to the

20th, and now the 21st. You see more things per minute than someone who's walking at the normal amble. Plus you're more removed from the world around you. The *flâneur* can be, and indeed tries to be, mistaken for someone out on an errand, albeit in no hurry. A jogger looks like a jogger.

In Cairo, before I discovered it was more fun to run by the Nile, I ran on the dusty horse track of the Gezira Sporting Club on a huge tract of land on an island in the middle of the river. Over the end of the track loomed the approach to one of the Nile bridges that intersected the loop, though in a higher plane. Most of the loop, the part closest to the buildings, was wide, so that I could imagine horses running on it. But in the shadow of the highway, the dirt that exhaled puffs of gray under my feet dwindled to a single lane, went around a broken fence, and made me wonder how anyone, man or horse, could properly make the whole loop. Perhaps the fly-over looming above simply stopped traffic below.

Many neighborhoods in Cairo had these surreal fly-overs to Nile bridges apparently planned well after the buildings and leaving whole worlds in their shadows that were usually used as car parks, or in some cases were only tortuous pedestrian mazes involving illegal cross-overs, tiny islands between two directions of chaotic traffic, and fences not meant to be traversed, requiring crossing traffic with no light (you hold out your hand at the rushing cars, as if this alone would dissuade them) up to the end of an illegal island, and then making your way along the curb down to another place where you can cross, taking your life in your outstretched hand.

The Gezira Sporting Club was a time warp of its own, with its height-of-chic-in-1955 leatherette chairs in a no-atmosphere clubhouse embalmed by the smugness of its own exclusivity. Nonetheless there was a croquet lawn, a small putting green, and places to sit outside under the palm trees—all of it offering a less expansive feeling than the comparable club in Bombay, where the sheer emptiness of the playing fields in this chaotic city were what made the layout so surreal, an island of tranquility off the teeming, pullulating streets. But Cairo isn't Bombay: the streets do not pullulate to quite so great a degree with people, beggars are few, and the river is nearby with its balustrades like dusty unkempt versions of Roman walkways along the river, flowing along considerably lower down, to offer open space. Cairo is not a ruin, as Calcutta—another city that springs to mind for comparison—seems to the Westerner; instead it's a world inhabited by people who don't seem to get the point, or with other things on their mind. Trees do not, by and large, grow from the roofs of seemingly abandoned buildings in Cairo, as they do in Indian cities; yet an ugly gray concrete slab building will have been shoved in on one side of a decrepit villa, and another on the other side; an arcade once meant to mimic the Rue de Rivoli will have been cut off after only an arch or two to allow taller, uglier buildings to intrude.

Along the Nile embankments are parked huge restaurant boats that give an air of nightlife gaity to this part of town near Zamalek: here are the few belly-dancers, now almost exclusively foreigners, that still ply their trade in this newly prudish Cairo where women wear head scarves, one in twenty is swathed in black, and some wear the Iranian version with an eye slit and long shining gloves that makes them look like a combination of a nun, a carnival participant, and a woman in evening clothes. Some of the boats, moored by the wall, have many smaller restaurants, like floating food courts: there are colorful signs along the sides of the boats, which are connected to the sidewalk by long protected gangplanks. At this hour of the morning, all are shut, yet none have cleaned up from their work the night before. Catering wagons are parked at the curb, and I have to thread around them; the ground is littered with wilted cabbage leaves, odd carrots, and pieces of paper. The soldiers who protect them, sitting back in chairs at the entrances to the boats and toting AK-47s, stifle yawns here in the gray dawn.

I run over a bridge. There are some isolated vehicles, but I see them coming from far away. I stop a moment in the center to look down at the sluggish, dark water. The sun is up, but only barely, and the air is still vibrant with mystery, something it will begin to lose as the light strengthens. I touch the nose of the lion on the pilaster at the side of the bridge and turn up the other side, toward Garden City and the Hyatt, on its little island closer to the other, eastern, bank of the river.

Most of the buildings here are at least scuffed, many are decrepit. On my way back I overshoot my hotel on purpose to walk back in a cool off, walking by relics of the British: "Pyramid House" is my favorite, its name spelled out in discolored Art Deco letters from the 1930s, though it's nowhere near the pyramids, washing hanging from its balconies with their view of the stagnant Nile below, echoing the equally sluggish Tiber in Rome. The building façades are spotted with age and falling plaster. This is a dry heat; things corrode more slowly than in the active rottenness of, say, Calcutta—where I never had the nerve to run, as the sidewalks are so full of holes, the people in such swarms—or degenerate by flaking off rather than growing mold and turning rancid. The cars puff huge clouds of dark white smoke; the gasoline, I am told, is still leaded. This must take its toll on the buildings too. I have read that Cairene policemen have the highest levels of lead in their blood of any group of people in the world.

In Alexandria, the Mediterranean city a train ride away from Cairo, I run at daybreak along the slick wave-spattered stones of the Corniche, watching the seedy buildings give way to the Tomb of the Unknown Soldier and then to the over-florid modern mosque, and then the stinking-of-fish fishermen's strip, past the excavations where the few tourists there are are invited to visit the underwater excavations of "Cleopatra's Palace"—the source of eerie photographs I later saw in the Alexandria National Museum, divers swimming around statues holding out their hands as if to the fish circling around them, their heads cocked as if seeing something on the ocean floor. The paving stones were wet and the wind was so strong that it had deformed the stunted palms planted at intervals between the stones into permanently hunched small shapes, protected by rush matting that had bent in the direction of the wind. I circle the Qait Bey fortress, built—so tradition has it—from the stones of the celebrated Lighthouse of Alexandria. The stones are slick from the spray that crashes against the jetty.

Later, when the sun is fully up, I re-trace my running route in a mini-van taxi. In the mini-vans of about a dozen seats in several rows here is quite a developed etiquette, I realize when I get in an almost full one and try to sit further forward than the backmost empty seat: I am waved back, back. Then there's the money ballet. People hand their folded over and apparently much-used single pound (20 cent) notes forward by sticking out their arms. The people in the seat in front of them take the money and pass it on without looking at the source of this little piece of greasy paper suddenly hovering by their face. They hand up their fare in the same fashion in conventional, larger busses, the ride a constant flight of moving bits of paper, being transferred from the black-shrouded women to the normal-looking men, so that finally they end up with the money taker, far in the back of the bus. Why don't they pay the driver, or the money-taker, as you get on? Perhaps because the human interaction would be lost.

Apparently these waves of money-passing are the way public transportation works. Back in Cairo, I take a trip out to the Pyramids on a proper bus where I stand, but am too tall to have much of a view outside, my head protruding into the covered part of the bus. All I can see is the continuous wave of money changing hands just below my eye-level while the people look elsewhere and go on with their conversations. And then suddenly everyone get out, in a village. Before us, abruptly, are the Pyramids. And then the desert starts. You can't run in the desert.

A tourist policeman sits on a camel silhouetted against the Pyramid of Cheops. Two American girls clown for photographs inside the nearby tomb of a lesser but still important functionary. The Sphinx (as the Greeks called it; there's apparently no evidence it was such to the Egyptians) is covered with birds that make its head look as if dotted with the remains of plugs of hair, like the head of too dearly loved dolly my wife has saved from her childhood, and that I finally put a hospital newborn knit hat on to hide the broken off tufts. Down the hill and past the Sphinx, the road turns touristy: there are many groups of school girls, all with colorful scarves over their hair, and pre-adolescent boys. All say "Hello where are you from?" or "Hello what's your name?." I smile and wave. I wish I'd remembered my hat. I'm sweating, and it's only mid-March. The dust has already begun to turn the green leaves of the trees beside the road the gray color of lizard's eyes. It is the brief Egyptian spring; soon summer will start. And then there will be no more running.

Cairo or Lone Pine, I have made these things comprehensible by covering great distances in open spaces at times where life has not really started: I have established intimacy by taking advantage of the fact that most of the time in the world, nobody is watching. Not even in densely populated urban areas—if you do your running at the right time. So the things are there for me to glean.

Treadmill

Gleaning requires that runners take advantage of the naturally fallow times and places of the world. If you run during work hours, everyone is up, and probably you have to compete with other people going about their business.. Beginnings and ends of days are best. We have to pick our spaces just the way we have to pick our times. It's best when we can run through open spaces, which usually means empty roads and parks with unplanned space, or local tracks when the team isn't on them: in these cases, I'm both part of the world and beyond it. Nobody wants these things, it seems, at least not right now: nobody begrudges them to me.

Yet running at odd times of day is not the only way to fit in a run. Many people sign up for races because the race, with its public preparation and the streets closed on the day of the race to allow the passage of the runners, makes it clear that the running is both rule and exception. Organized races make holidays of the act of running: they're both special and part of the normal round. People make way for runners in a race; races solve the problem of the relation between life and what transcends it by acknowledging the problem as unsolvable: you just have to give in to the divide.

Running on a treadmill in a gym or in the basement marries life to what transcends it too. Here, the exceptionable is made unexceptional: what else are you supposed to do with a treadmill, after all, but run on it? There's the machine, and we're servicing it. Of course, the movement on a treadmill takes some getting used to. Your body moves in a fundamentally different way on a moving band than on the non-moving ground: on the rubber surface of a treadmill you're trying to keep your lower body from being swept away beneath you, as if you were battling against a current in the water—the principle of the stationary swimming pool, a bathtub with a current, that is the swimming equivalent of a treadmill.

Running outside to cover ground, on your own time and in public places, is different because you can stop, or slow to a walk: your speed is something you decide to add. On a treadmill you're forced to battle the beast: if you stop, you die. Of course it's a fictitious contest: you can always hit the button that says "Stop" and the motion under your feet slows. But so long as we engage in the combat we have to concentrate: on a treadmill we're typically counting minutes, or calories, or parts of a program: we're conscious at every moment. The treadmill makes the goal movement for a certain time, or a certain pulse level, or a certain program of bars on the monitor. The goal is no longer running for its own sake.

Outside, it is. On a familiar route, or a repetitive one, we can blur out our surroundings and concentrate only on the sensation of moving our body on its drifting axis, as if our limbs were a sort of unfolded gyroscope, flapping on our center like a butterfly rather than circling it in a whir. The primary challenge of running outdoors isn't conquering the ground, or shouldn't be. Indeed under the best of circumstances it doesn't feel like a challenge at all. It feels instead the way it felt, as a child, to be given a pocketful of change at the fair and sent free, told to come back when we'd spent it all. We have the energy for a certain amount; we know we're going to spend it. The only question is how. We get the satisfaction of spending it as we wish (speed up here? take it slower?) but also the reminder of limitation in the satisfying tiredness we sense at the end, the feeling that we've done as much as we could but now we have, at least for a while, no more to give. Sprinting the final bit helps convince ourselves we've calibrated the energy expenditure correctly. We can use up what we have left, and come home with empty pockets.

3
Running in the Adirondacks

One summer evening I sat on the porch at my mother's house in the Adirondacks, looking through the gap in the trees down at the lake. The white birch trees glowed against the pines, and the lake, visible only in a chink through the trees, shimmered blue with the oblique sun. Inside the house, on the other side of the sliding glass door that closed off the porch, my children watched a video; I heard the faint risings and fallings of its high-pitched sounds, muted by distance and glass.

Behind me on Route 9, hidden visually but not aurally behind a fringe of trees—whose bottom branches have died either as a result of old age and natural processes or as a result of the salt that's dumped on the major roads in the winter—I could hear the passage of an occasional truck or the fainter sound of a car, though the noise was obscured by being on the other side of the house, by the trees, and by being above the roof line of the house, built on a slope down to the lake that continued before my eyes—not to mention being muffled by long familiarity. Down toward the lake, I could see a small strip of the dirt road between the house and the lake, the road I run on.

The house is set in a cleared-out space in the trees. The next house over is lived in only on weekends: the people have two teen-aged boys, and though I can't see the house for trees, everything that's said there comes through loud and clear. We can sit on my mother's porch and listen to their discussions, the warp and woof of family life, the boys' teen-aged speech of someone being "all like" this and "all like" that, the father's "five minute warning" then "one minute warning" to prepare them for coming in or dinner, their discussions of sports teams. Yet they're invisible, their lives simultaneously laid open to scrutiny and completely hidden. When I see this family it is only briefly, from the road, requiring a long loop around, and it requires an effort of imagination to connect them with the disembodied but so personal voices that filter through the trees.

Owen and Teddy, my sons, have a tree house in the woods between these two houses. The tree house was built by the previous owners for their grandchildren, who rarely visited. Its roof is a sheet of plywood on which the pine needles accumulate, so that it's warped and close to punching through in places, the result of many years of rain and rot. For a time the piece of wood over the door read "Alexandra's Tree House," for my autistic daughter, now close to adulthood, who started coming up here with me when she was still of an age when she could conceivably have been interested. But like so many things we tried to interest her in, it never took. She came up once or twice, said "Oh" in the tone of voice she had learned to imitate that said interest, and then never went up again. Now I've made a new sign that says "Owen and Teddy's Tree House." They love it. One day they insisted on eating their lunch in the tree house, and my mother made up lunches in brown paper bags. They marched across the grass with their lunches and determined expressions.

It was down by the lake, Loon Lake (one of 29 in the Adirondacks with this name), on a bench that has since been replaced with another, that I asked my wife to marry me. I wrote a poem about this that I read at our wedding. It talked about running along this dust-fine road, and walking there with her in the dark of night (it was just after midnight when I proposed), negotiating the bumps by memory. For us, now, this dock is merely the place where the boys jump off for their swims. Still, the events of the past have over-layered on the present. The same place has been visited under many circumstances. Now I am back with my wife, my daughter, and my two boys. We wonder how many years my mother, in her mid-80s, will be able to come to this house, which we call "The House in the Woods," though my house in Maryland is in almost as much woods as this one.

Some things change between visits to the lake, but the effect on us, coming only once a year and at the same season of changeless summer, is to suggest that things stay the same. My mother's house has, to be sure, undergone the repairs of all houses, especially those in the Adirondacks, with its extremes of cold and hot, wet and dry. It's gotten a new roof, been painted all over at least once, acquired a room off to one side so well integrated that the viewer wouldn't be able to say it hadn't always been there, and (invisible from the outside) had its downstairs bedroom redone twice, including getting new carpets, drywall and paneling, due to a malfunctioning sump pump that flooded the carpets and the lower parts of the walls. Yet we're not usually the ones here to make these changes: we tend to see only the result, or the status quo restored. It seems as if we come to the lake to measure our changes against a standard, a sort of Greenwich hour or yardstick that itself never changes. That's also how E.B. White saw his summer vacations he wrote about in his essay "Once More to the Lake," about a place that, save for small details, didn't seem to change—until the moment he realized he'd replaced his father and his son, his younger self. No change, then the jump of a generation. Our own worlds back home, away from the lake, seem less static, but also lack such great jumps. We accept the slow creep of changes that would shock a Rip van Winkle who had missed twenty years.

Even at the lake abrupt changes are possible, and if we came more often and at different times of year we'd be more conscious of them. The lake could be drained between one visit and another—indeed it is drained in the fall, more water is allowed over its dam (it's really a dammed-up river, not a true lake). Or there can be sudden changes with the float the children swim out to and dive off —it'll be there all summer, then one day not: inside of ten minutes when it's hauled up, things change utterly. Someone in one of the houses might have died since the last visit—death is an abrupt change that somehow we get used to—or the house itself been bashed in by a falling tree. If all these things happened at once we'd buzz with conversation: so many changes! But it would be coincidence, and the causality is in the opposite direction: we comment on things that seem abnormal, it's not the commenting on them that makes them so. Still, focused on our own world as we are and less conscious of the neighbors than we might be, changes seem minor.

What we call "change" is an effect of our noticing something, and noticing something is determined by what we know. Change at all means not the usual; major changes means, not the usual size of change. By definition major changes happen seldom; if they happened more often they wouldn't be major, but minor.

Loops

Running here at the lake offers the same alternation of minor change and major continuity as our once-a-year visits to the lake, or indeed of what we use to measure repetitive cycles in life itself: five loops around, each one the same and, in minor particulars, each one different, with my reaction to the changes based on what experience has prepared me for. I know what comes next, where the dips and hollows are, how many steps it takes to get up what hill. This knowledge is of no use to anyone who doesn't run or walk this loop: if ever I cease to run here, the knowledge will die with me. Still, for now it's important information. I can visualize every rise and fall, know what I'm going to see at every turn.

It takes twelve breaths to get up the initial low-rise rise past the neighbor's house and the chalet with the red geraniums in the boxes that looks down the hill to the closer lake access, where I asked Meg to marry me. I start counting at the foot of the hill, just opposite a large tree. The largest hill, near the end, can be measured a couple of ways. It's almost halfway around the loop, on the ascent back up to the road level. The hill proper begins when I turn the corner just beyond the house where the construction has been going on for years. I begin counting when I'm going uphill, not in the middle of the 90 degree turn. I look at the ground for the first ten breaths, and concentrate on staying in the middle of the road, where the crest is highest and the road not on a sideways incline. By about breath 12 or 13 I allow myself to look up; I can see the top of the hill at this point. A good run is 40 breaths to the large stone, and 50 to the ridge just beyond that where the road briefly descends and where I turn around and run backwards. At 70 breaths, I'm on a flat area and I turn again and run up the lesser hill on the other side to the tree, by which point I can be either at 100 or 105, depending on whether it's the first loop or the last, or a good day or a bad.

I then have the option of running the small slope down to the road backwards or forwards (backwards is better for knees), during which I usually think about the annual rummage sale that takes place right here by this short section of dirt road down to Rt. 9, as well as meditate on the renters who are sometimes in this A-frame house on the corner who fly the Swiss flag (though I learned at one Homeowner's Association that they're not Swiss nor have any association with Switzerland), the large house across the road which used to belong to an old lady who ran an antique shop out of one large room of the house (now it's said CLOSED across the dusty window for years, during which I haven't seen any sign of her, and the gravel driveway is filled with cars from New Jersey and some with New York plates, presumably her children who now come to use the house), and the entrance posts to the development by the lake, where the pushy neighbor who now is in the hospital with a heart attack tried to get the Homeowner's Association to put lamps on top, and was defeated.

Every step of the running loop is thus over-layered with associations, trivial though they are. The first house on the left used to be lived in by people from New Jersey whom we used to see down on the beach; they sold it and now I don't know who's in it. That's opposite the place with the sign that used to say "Grandpa's Camp" and now says "Great-Grandpa's Camp," where Great-Grandpa is the old man with the large dog whose poop he refuses to pick up, though the rules say he has to. On the first hill, my daughter learned to ride a bicycle, much later than most children (she's hardly ridden since), and the first time went careening down the hill and fell off. At the end of the part of the road that skirts the lake, a garage has been under construction for several seasons without seeming to make much progress: the surprise here is not that it changes, but that it doesn't. We know what the speed of such things is, and this isn't right.

Sometimes there are changes from one loop of the five-loop run to the next, comparable to the changes from one year's visit to the lake to the next year's: changes in the way I'm feeling, a leaf that's fallen, my own tracks that weren't there before. I only notice the things that seem out of place: I wouldn't stop on seeing a leaf on loop three where none had been on loop two, but I'd certainly remark a tree that had fallen. I learn what will be there the next time and what won't: I leave the birch bark I intend to bring home for my son by the side of the path because I know it will be there the next loop, and the next. However I don't look at the next loop for the butterfly that rests briefly on the sand before me. Unless, of course, it's dead, in which case I do.

The last, largest hill, is the real indicator of change: whether or not I run it easily allows me to say where I am in my visit—typically runs on the first day aren't so good, as this is the mountains—and how I'm feeling: easy means I've been getting enough sleep, hard means I haven't. Other changes and variations include how rutted the sand is from rain. Sometimes there's an ineffective portable rubber speed bump opposite the tree, though it's pulled away or disappears altogether in the off-season and other times simply disappears mysteriously.

Surprise, say at something that didn't typically happen between one loop and the next, only means surprise; it needn't mean there's something wrong with the world, only that I noted the change and found it unexpected. Besides, surprise is a specific point on a spectrum that stretches from mildly puzzled to truly flummoxed. If a tree branch is lying on the path between one loop and the next, I may be startled but I'm probably not surprised: it probably fell, I'd think, and continue running. If it's a large tree, or more startlingly still, a large tree cut into neat firewood pieces between one loop and the next, I'd be flummoxed: how could people have moved this quickly, and without me hearing their power saws? (Perhaps it's not wood from this tree, and the saws had silencers, and they worked quickly: it's part of a movie shoot, perhaps—only there's no movie crew around.) But what if a large tree is *growing* from the path between one loop and the next? This one requires serious head-scratching. We don't know. Perhaps we've taken a wrong turning without paying attention? Surprise merely means we're on our way to being better informed. It's not the world that has to adapt, but us.

Sometimes it's not the individual changes that surprise us, but the rate at which they arrive. If the changes come more intensely or thicker than is usual, we're upset—but this difficulty is only because of what we're used to, not the intrinsic speed of the change. If we have problems with job, health, and children all in a few weeks, we say we're in a high-stress period, and perhaps "seek counseling," something we don't do for a change that we find more normal, such as a wrinkle or a child's lost tooth. Or the speed of a change we're used to varies: if we turn gray (as we say) "overnight" (though usually this is within some months) it's commented on, not least of all by us. Things aren't supposed to happen this way.

The change that happens on my run at the expected rates isn't even usually registered as change: I don't register any trees in different places between one loop and the next, so I say their location hasn't changed; I'm not looking at the dust in the road, so I don't register the changes there. But we've learned to focus on what doesn't change in ten minutes between loops—the trees—and not on what does, say the patterns in the dust beneath my feet. That way we don't have to spend all our time processing change.

We have many locutions for change to which we're accustomed. In the individual, these are expressed in the following way, among others: I got a craving for, I decided that, I gave myself permission for, I suddenly realized that X, I found myself thinking about, obsessed with, or "over" Y. In the world outside ourselves, things are no different: most changes are merely accepted without our asking for an explanation. The world still jerks from one state to the next, but we're not upset by the jerk.

I lack an explanation as to why the leaf is on the path (I would assume it had fallen, but if it's green that might seem strange: maybe somebody climbed up and got it and then placed it here; maybe it's a bomb; and so on) but that's the end of my deliberation: I merely leave the situation and move on, identifying the jerk without seeking an explanation. This is no different from not having an explanation as to why I suddenly want chocolate rather than vanilla. I say that I "want" one rather than the other and that's that. Nobody asks for justification, not even us. That's the nature of the subjective: it's a realm where no one cares. If someone does care, however (*why* do you want chocolate rather than vanilla?) we move this from the subjective to the objective realm, and develop vocabulary (that of psychology and medicine, most likely) to probe it. That someone can be ourself.

This is a fundamental shift, between merely perceiving the world and questioning it, accepting it as it is and trying to explain it. This shift may be related to the split between the self and others, but it is not congruent to this second shift. We can ask for explanation when we're alone, or with others; the impetus for asking for explanations is not always other people—unless we say this is true by definition. Thus it is not true that only other people ask for explanations, and therefore the division between ourself and others is not the primary one in our situation of being in the world. More fundamental is the split between questioning something and not questioning something, between being in direct relationship with the world and being alienated from it.

It's not change itself that surprises us, only abnormal change, a sort of second-order change. Right now Owen is growing about three inches a year: we try on pants from him last season and realize we have to give Teddy this pair. We expect this, and it doesn't shock us. But if he grew six inches a year, it might. We aren't surprised by the over-weeks-or-months growth of plants because we know it will happen; the sudden in-one-night appearance of mushrooms or, in the tropics, the shooting-up of banana trees, may still be something we note, though it's not something we ask for explanation for: we know why it happens, mushrooms and banana trees grow at that rate, though other plants don't. But great would be the surprise occasioned by a pine or birch tree shooting up six feet overnight. Yet if all plants grew at the rate of mushrooms, we wouldn't be surprised, and what to us is a normal plant that takes weeks or months to form would seem surprisingly slow.

We don't expect people to grow third arms, so if they did, that would surprise us. But we do expect changes that to an outsider to the human race might well seem equally startling: we expect children to grow taller, their faces to thin out, their teeth to fall out and be replaced—and then with time, we expect the arrival of gray hair and the wrinkles. One by one, so that we have time to get used to them.

All surprise is the result of our expectations being contravened. And as a result of being surprised, we may look for or demand an explanation. Is the arm (or as we may say, convinced it's not real, the "apparent" arm) glued on, and hence not "grown" in the sense we mean it? Is it the arm from a vestigial Siamese twin inside? We can only suggest the explanations we're aware of: in other cases we merely set out to find one. Perhaps we find it, perhaps we don't. Many explanations are possible, but all presuppose both our being surprised and demanding an explanation. This demand is not itself in need of explanation any more than it needs it.

Miracles

This situation is one that has caused much ink to be spilled, with scientific types insisting that there are some things so unlikely they'll never happen (or indeed, *cannot* happen)—such as a person actually growing a viable third arm as we watch—and religious sorts insisting that for God, anything is possible. This is the strange debate about whether or not miracles are possible.

What's strange about it is that both sides are in agreement about 99.99% of the issue, so that the ferocity of the argument is determined precisely by the statistical irrelevance of what is being argued about, and the fact that both sides are trying to get an explanation for something that by definition can't have one. Both sides in this argument agree that a person apparently growing a third arm as we watch is at least highly unlikely, just as both sides agree that having all doctors say that someone has two days to live means it is at least highly unlikely that he will live twenty years. Both sides, that is, agree that experience can teach us that X is far more certain than not: perhaps that "third arms don't grow as we watch because bodies don't grow that way and at that rate"; perhaps that "when the body is ravaged by cancer it can't survive."

Yet of course our certainty or near certainty that this case will turn out a certain way is based on many presuppositions, any one of which could be wrong. Most basically, we believe that the case we see before us *is* such a case as the one that is so certain. Thus we presuppose that we saw what we thought we saw. Perhaps we didn't; perhaps the apparent growth of a third arm on the person was in fact the result of a skillfully projected movie done on a computer, or the arm was a rubber inflatable. So if something we think impossible happens, we typically look for ways to say, what has happened isn't the impossible thing, but something else. This isn't what we meant by, say, "growing a third arm."

Which is to say: if it's possible, it's not what we meant. However that doesn't show it can't apparently happen in front of us. Perhaps this person turns out to be a Martian, and it turns out Martians can grow third arms. In a narrow sense we'd still be right: people can't grow third arms. Or it's an arm but not a viable one, like the vestigial third feet of some chicks that dangle helplessly. So we say, yes, he's a person, but it's not an arm, not the way we mean it. People with this sort of cancer almost always die, only it turned out the person didn't have this sort, or we forgot to say (because we didn't know) that people with this sort of cancer *and no contrary factors mitigating it* (such as this person, unbeknownst to us, had) always die, and so on.

Yet even skeptics give up sometime—at least, most skeptics. Let's say the arm is flesh and blood, touching it is touching the person, X-rays reveal it is part of the same skeleton and so on. Perhaps it's a mutation that has simply never happened before? Or was misperceived when it did, or labeled differently or not at all? (This is Michel Foucault's position with regard to mental illness: the state existed before the Enlightenment, but did not have a name and so was tolerated as a series of individual variations, rather than being a separate category that required a separate way of treating these people.)[10] If someone refused to give in and agree that what was seen was a disproof, most people would move on, relegating that person to an individual kook. This doesn't mean this person is wrong in continuing to insist that this just can't be a counter-example; just that most people don't care enough to follow his or her lead.

Religious types want to insist that there is no scientific law or rule so absolute that God can't overturn it. But they are in agreement with the scientist that there is a degree of knowledge about the world so compelling that the probability of this case not being an example of it is so small it would require a "miracle." an end to the process of asking for explanation (on the grounds that we've found it: God). Let's say the cancer patient who was sure to die recovers. The scientist may shrug and speak of factors at work we haven't yet discovered. The priest says no: it has been found, and this we call "the will of God." The scientist can continue to insist the explanation exists, though s/he may never find it. There is only an argument so long as it's not found.

The priest and the scientist don't, most fundamentally, disagree, they agree. First of all, they agree about the limiting case that is the only place we can even speak of a "miracle." If the doctors agree that the chances of survival are 50-50—which means simply that we don't know whether the patient will survive or not—then it's by definition not a miracle if the patient survives. Nor is it a miracle that a minor operation is a minor operation and the patient survives fine: the chances were 99% of this happening, after all. Nor is it a miracle that my shoes are where I left them, or that my tea cup holds my coffee, and so on—here the probability is very great as well. For the priest to maintain a miracle has happened, all knowledge has to point to X happening, and yet it doesn't. And oh yes, the X is a bad thing: we never say God performed a miracle by having the patient in a minor operation he was supposed to survive die on the operating table.

Thus even a miracle in the priest's sense is determined by what we know, and this is accepted by both sides. It's only in situations where both sides agree we know the maximum we can know that the concept of a miracle is even invoked. It's as if even the priest says God lets science do its thing up to the very limit, and then reserves the right to step in. By definition this stepping in would be beyond the limits of science, so how can science say it can't happen? By the same token it's so rare that strong knowledge fails to describe the result, why is the priest so concerned to insist that it is possible? Sure it's possible. It's just so unlikely as to be something we can't count on.

Some people will say: science teaches us more than that there is *some* explanation. It teaches us that the explanation must be *of a certain sort*, part of the natural world. If all of a sudden the tree isn't there between one loop and the next, that's unexpected, so it seems to require an explanation. (If between one year and the next it isn't there, by contrast, I probably won't ask for an explanation as I'll assume I know what it is—someone cut it down and hauled it away, and the leaves have covered over the spot.) But we'd say: at least we know it didn't "just disappear" and it wasn't "taken away by elves." We're very proud that we can eliminate some causes: the supernatural, say. Or perhaps even that God had the whim to make it disappear, so He did.

But this isn't denying some explanations as valid, it's saying that some things aren't explanations. If there are no elves, then it's not okay to say that elves took it away, any more than it is to say that a Shazam took it away. What's a Shazam? There is no Shazam. So we're not saying anything by saying we want a "scientific" explanation, only that we want an explanation, and that the others don't qualify.

But when we say the tree didn't "just disappear," we mean that we're unaware that a tree can be gone in a micro-second, whereas it can be gone over an afternoon. But maybe we just aren't aware of the way a tree can be made to be gone in a micro-second: probably the people on whom the atomic bombs were dropped would have said this series of events was impossible too.

Even ascribing an event to the occurrence of a miracle is to note it as exceptional and demand an explanation. Most of the world passes with no demand for an explanation at all—so the priest needs miracles to proves God's intervention in the world, by definition God is all but absent. God in this sense is an explanation, and most things do not require them, neither scientific nor religious in nature.

We rarely ascribe a tree's not turning colors, during the period when typically they don't—say high summer—to God's intervention: if something proceeds as expected, we don't need an explanation at all. This may be that it changes on cue (the turning of the seasons, say or the loss of a child's teeth) or that it doesn't change when in fact we have no reason to expect a change: my fingers aren't an inch shorter than they were a moment ago. Yet they may be a bit drier, or greasier—something for which we don't ask for an explanation. The more profound point about explanation is not the relatively small variation between explanation by natural forces on one hand and God on the other, but rather the fact that we only ask for explanation at all when we're surprised, and we're only surprised when we're surprised. And what's the explanation for that? God? The natural world? We're not prepared to say. We can't explain what undergirds all explanation: its shifts and changes are not themselves amenable to explanation.

Graduation
Most of the time we fail to ask for explanations because we know how things work: leaves fall, even green ones, and lots of brown ones in autumn. When we turn the key in the ignition the car starts. When we say "please" people smile at us or give us what we want: we know how the world works. It's rare when we don't, and this by definition: we're surprised by the unexpected. Other people are part of the expected, so the most fundamental distinction is not between ourselves and others, but between what surprises us and what doesn't, and what we ask for explanations of and what we at least think we understand:

the known merging with the unknown. Demands for explanation come from our own placement of ourselves among others, subjective melding into objective: we want to understand and colonize a world that we do not yet know, make outside our own.

We inhabit the rhythm of our lives: even departures from this rhythm are departures only because of what we take for granted. All of our reactions are within the closed loops of what we know and so expect. We celebrate the milestones we celebrate: for us they have meaning. There's no such thing as absolute triumph or failure: our triumphs are triumphs only to us, within the context of our lives; our failures only failures relative to ourselves. Do we look young for our age? Presumably we're pleased. Ten years younger? Is that remarkable? How about the people who are ten years younger than we: are they remarkable? And when we are ten years older will we look the age we really now are? And will that be remarkable too?

We are caught in our own lives, as I am in my own run, even unto the diversions from the expected part of the pattern: there's no way to pull ourselves up by our own bootstraps in life. Our pleasures are got by contrast with what we're used to (we got a bargain! we graduated! the last hill was easier than usual!), our disappointment the result of what we'd hoped for (I wanted to win the lottery but didn't; I was slower today than the last time). We define tragedy as being something worse than the norm, and celebrate things better than the norm. If the norm were different than it is, we'd celebrate something different, mourn other things.

Centaur

Running loops around the lake, noting when I am surprised and when not, makes clear the problem of Kant, who was responding to Empiricists like John Locke.

Locke held that what we have in our heads is only what we've perceived: from this came his doctrine of the blank slate at birth, the *tabula rasa*. A centaur is imagined only by putting together parts of the things we've imagined. To this responded Kant, conceding the point while undermining it: of course what we perceive, the content, comes from living. But the form of perception—that is more fundamental—is something we're born with. To which I say, perhaps along with Wittgenstein: if we can talk about this form, it has precise qualities. And this means, it isn't something that underlies all we do, but a precise thing. And if it's a precise thing, then we can do or be another precise thing: this is how we can contravene or neutralize or render trivial any "fundamental form." Anything you can talk about is part of life, not something beyond it.

To this Kant, far from giving up, would say: your very disagreement presupposes my forms. Without them you can't even respond. You can disagree, but your disagreement proves my point.

Yet if everything we do, or rather the fact of doing it, proves Kant's point, then there's also no point in his making that point, or in writing or reading the books that set it out. It gives us nothing more than we already have to have the principles of things articulated if really they are exemplified by every aspect of the world we live in. Failing to articulate them also, in that case, exemplifies them, as does denying them: so a world of people who had never thought to articulate these things is just as acceptable as a world of those who agree with Kant, and a world of Lockes, who disagree with Kant, is also just as acceptable. So why do we need Kant at all?

But if it somehow does change things to have them articulated—if doing so makes, say, Newtonian science possible, or justifies it, as Kant's *Critique of Pure Reason* is held to have done—then it's clear that these fundamental rules weren't the underlying principles of (so to speak) all music, but rather a melody produced by one man on one instrument. The more fundamental things are, the less relevant they are to the world, because they underlie the contrary of anything we say or do as well as what we are trying to promote. Thus Kant's doctrine of the forms of apperception is part of the world, rather than something underlying it: it's part of the history of philosophy, one more overbalance, not the end of the stacking process. This is Wittgenstein's point: if you can talk about something, it's part of the world, the transcendent is the here and now. So there may be fundamental forms that transcend particulars, for all we know. But if they really are fundamental, by definition we'll never grasp them, because every situation is particular. This is the gap Plato filled with his notion of "contemplating" forms: it's a postulate rather than something we know to be possible.

The default situation of the world is not the demand for explanation, but the situation where the world conforms to our expectations to the point where we don't think to ask for an explanation. In this state the self merges with others, subjective with objective. And why should the world not conform to our expectations? Those expectations were founded on the world. We don't think about the fact that when we pick up our right foot the shoe comes with it, but we'd notice and probably be exasperated if the shoe remained stuck to the ground. We don't notice that depressing the keys on the computer make these letters, but we'd notice if one skipped. We don't notice that the level of tea in our cup is (we'd think) still where it was the last time we took a sip (we don't notice this small an amount of evaporation), but we'd notice if it were empty or the level appreciably lower. We don't notice that putting on a coat makes us warmer, but we'd notice if it made us colder. This is the vast underlayer of the world that is as we expect it to be, and for this we typically do not ask for explanation. To ask for explanation we need some disconnect: others see it differently than we do, we ourselves experience conflicting desires, we see the situation as if from outside. Thus there is a large proportion of the world where words, philosophy, and reasoning hold no sway: we fail to see this to the degree that we consider only the problematic times of life, not the unproblematic.

Autism

If we see the leaf on the path or the dust re-arranged no more than dust normally is, we are not surprised, we merely run on. If there is a tree growing out of the path between one loop and the next, we are probably surprised, and in all probability ask for explanation. However the point at which we ask for explanation is itself variable. Some people are much more passive in the world than others. Alexandra, for instance, fails to ask "why?" in many situations that would cause a non-autistic person to pose that question: for her, to a large degree, things merely are as they are—that's the nature of autism, always being lost among the trees and never conceiving of the forest. Even non-autistic people arrange along a spectrum or more curious to less. We ask for explanation, or we don't: we're the end of the line on this, no principle can tell us what to do.

The tree at the foot of the hill may in fact turn from green to brown or red in one loop around the path: our not expecting it isn't going to stop it from happening. If this does happen, we may demand an explanation, or we may not: this is a fact about us, not the world. And we may get an explanation, or not. The world isn't responsible for having us understand it. First comes the change, then our sense that we have an explanation (which may be wrong) or not. I see a leaf in a different position on the path, or new tracks, or a tree has fallen, a house imploded in the fifteen minutes it takes to do a loop: at any of these it may be I don't know why, and set out to figure out. The world outside is in this way the same as the world inside, shot through with things we don't have an explanation for. Whether or not we look for such explanation is not something that, as a general phenomenon, can be explained.

This is the situation of being without explanation for explanation (or its lack) that's acted out in the drama of running. Nobody is making us run, unless it is ourselves, or as we may wish to argue others' desires and wishes as channeled through ourselves. If the question is, Should I run? there's no clear way to answer it. Based on what? Our own desires? What others say? Just as little is there an answer, if we do not see it already, to the question, Is this a thing that requires explanation? It's not clearly just a case of chocolate vs. vanilla, of saying "Sure, if you want to, do it; if not, don't"—because we may be overlooking things for which others will punish or criticize us (say a ticking bomb that we simply step over; in the case of running perhaps it sets a good example for our children, or makes us live longer).

There's no hard and fast answer to the question of whether something requires explanation or not, though all elements of the world are potentially relevant, if we choose to make them so. If the change is a leaf on the path we are likely to note it and move on without asking for explanation—unless the path is in the middle of a perfectly manicured and vast lawn with no trees. But even in the forest a leaf may excite interest: it's the wrong kind of tree (so maybe it was planted there by a criminal as a signal, a criminal who brought it in his pocket without knowing enough about trees to know that this leaf was not indigenous to this forest), or it's bright red in the dead of summer (so we would look around for a diseased tree: where could this have come from?). We can't say, since we're constantly caught on the interface between what we expect and what we see, and what we expect is determined by what we know.

Even this is not to vote with Locke against Kant: general rules may be one of the things we know, such as that men typically act in a certain way and women another, or that a hesitation before someone answers indicates that we shouldn't accept that person's response at face value, or that hair too dark for the condition of the skin almost certainly means dyed hair, or that time passes more slowly when you're eager for something to happen. Anything that can be articulated is something we can know and expect, even if we sub-divide the things we can know into forms and content. In some sense, all is content.

Inside the self

Still, it seems to some people that the self has to be constituted differently from the world outside: outside there's science, rules. Inside there's something else, call it "soul," that lacks rules. Inside we suddenly "decide" we'd rather have chocolate than vanilla, whereas we might hold that the world doesn't suddenly "decide" to let trees grow in the middle of the path where they didn't before, from one loop to the next. But it's not because we "suddenly decide X" that we're different than the world. Rather, we say we "suddenly decide X" because nobody, not even us, is interested in following it up, providing an explanation—whether because we think we know why, or we're just not interested (or others aren't). We can be objective with ourselves, and subjective in the world that contains others. If there's a leaf on the path between one loop and the next, we let it go without demanding an explanation: this is the equivalent of not asking why we suddenly "got a craving for X." There's change, but not change we're interested in explaining. Of course someone else, or a change of heart (note the locution) in ourselves, can impel us to deem this change puzzling enough to ask for an explanation—which doesn't mean we'll find one.

So the objective world isn't a place, it's a situation. It's the situation of demanding an explanation for something we don't expect—whereby the first step is usually to note the unexpected. We can find ourselves stuck between the objective and subjective worlds: we're aware of something that could be explained, only we don't know whether we're interested enough to ask for that explanation. Everything in the world can play a role in the transition from acceptance to questioning, but only after we have made this step. This is like saying that we can imagine everything we can imagine, but we cannot imagine the things we cannot imagine. We can never get an explanation for explanation, at least not one more general than a specific one.

We are the process of striving after fixity, perhaps achieving fixity fleetingly, and then continuing to run. This flickering back and forth between acceptance of the world and questioning of it, demanding explanation, is the relation of same and different in the loops around the lake. No one cares if I run here, no one cares if I run at all, yet I run in a public space in an objective world. Does it require explanation? Running on the edges of the day and the edges of society is a state between objective and subjective: it's in the world but nobody cares. We're alone, but in a social world. We're caught in a half-subjective, half-objective time and place, and hence in a half-subjective, half-objective state. We express both at the same time.

Pounding in the head

The decision to run or not run is typically a private one: nobody cares but us. Thus changes in this realm seem to be without explanation, rather like a craving for chocolate rather than vanilla. Yet that doesn't mean they're trivial changes. The way born-again Christians can remember the day of their enlightenment, so runners can invariably remember their turn-around, going from being non-runners to being runners. This reminds us that the part of life that has explanations is really quite small, largely because nobody asks for explanations for the rest: that's why running is so important. It's our own decision, and typically it lacks explanations.

For me this decision came the summer after I graduated from college. To be sure, there had been runs of a sort before that summer, back in 1974. But they had taken place years before, and under duress, and so they didn't count: they weren't in the realm where it's up to us, the chocolate vs. vanilla realm, but in the firmly objective realm. In high school, I was a year younger than everyone else, and so at a physical disadvantage. Every spring when the snow was barely melted, the boys' gym class would be herded outside, shivering in our shorts, to run a mile and a half around the track. I always got a stitch in my side and had to walk. I was the only one walking, which added to my shame. And finally I didn't have to take physical education, so I didn't. In absolute terms this can't have happened more than a small handful of times, perhaps 8th through 10th grades. But the experience was sufficiently mortifying and painful that I greeted the advent of spring with increasing dread: I was going to be sick. It wasn't until decades later that I could shed this association of physical illness with the first warming rays of March.

Mutatis mutandis, my high school was the one parodied in much more cleaned-up, better-funded versions in a hundred movies and teen musicals: all the students were walking Types—from the Geek to the Black Kid to the Jock to the Homecoming Queen. I was the Intellectual, editor of the literary magazine and co-editor of the newspaper, president of the French Club and the student "tolerance" club affiliated with the local NCCJ, the National Council of Christians and Jews. The rest of it was true to type too: the Homecoming King was the Quarterback, his queen was the Head Cheerleader, and so on, at James M. Bennett High School in Salisbury, Maryland. We know that in marriages frequently the couple polarizes, each becoming more so what he or she added to the combination, drifting from the center because there was a counterweight in the form of the other, who also drifts, only in the opposite direction. So it was with physicality and me back in high school: the popular kids were only physical, so I would be only mental.

This adoption of an extreme continued all through college: there, there was not so great a polarization, but once having adopted the anti-physical position, it had become a given of my being, something I would never have thought of questioning. I gained weight to the point of being able to pinch a roll around my middle; I spent all weekend in the library, going over Plato and Wittgenstein in search of a truth I finally had to admit was unattainable. There was no pressure to be physical, and I wasn't.

And then I graduated, out of school for the first time since I was three. Suddenly I was on my own, or rather, sort of on my own: I lived with my brother, my mother paid the bills. I wrote, all day every day, going to the library of the local university, the University of Maryland. My lunch was a thermos of coffee: I learned to love the feeling of hunger. My belly became flat. Yet one day, I was suddenly aware that I was breathing hard after walking up the three flights of stairs to the carrel I had claimed, by right of habit, as my own: I could hear my heart beating in my head, as if I were wearing a diver's helmet. This is where the change started that ended in my becoming a runner.

There are many more situations in the world that lack explanations than for which we seek them, even fewer for which we find them. That day in the library I abruptly realized that my aphysicality had been self-imposed, and further realized that, since I had imposed it, I could un-impose it. What I had thought was me suddenly seemed like a suit of clothing that I could put off. What caused this shift of perspective, this shift of my very nature? I don't know; just as little do I know whether I can even look for an explanation, and what sort it would be if I found it. That's Wittgenstein's "mystical," the thing that undergirds all action.

Indeed, there's no way to make a realization like this make sense outside of the context in which it occurred. How could I suddenly "see as" separable something that had not seemed so? What sense does the concept of "separable" make, given that it refers to the creature entertaining it? Why would something in one instant seem to be a part of ourselves and in the next moment not so? All realizations surge from darkness; all we can do is note the change, we can't run the line backwards into the obscurity.

I must have had this experience of breathlessness many times before. Why had I not drawn any conclusions? Why was it only now that I decided to took action, "gave myself permission" (as we say to show we have no idea why we didn't before) to change my life? Should I say, I wasn't ready to? It wasn't time? It wasn't meant to be? I had worked through the philosophy that prepared me for another kind of solution to life than words, found it wanting and was ready to come up on the other side? Why here? Why now? We can only say what happens, not why it didn't happen sooner, or at another time, or not at all.

Some Christian, and some Muslim, thinkers in the Middle Ages, held that God constantly re-created the world, which could end at any second. The Christian church resisted the march of science in the Renaissance: the world potentially fell apart at every moment, rather than being held together by natural laws. Nowadays we think these views outmoded, old-fashioned. I think they're common sense—that's what running suggests, at any rate.

Suddenly, in any case, I was ready to be physical. This could have been suggested to me a thousand times before, and probably had been, only I was not receptive. Now, I was, perhaps most of all because I was the one doing the suggesting (whatever this means). There are unseen patterns, it seems, in the human call-it-psyche, which either only come to exist when they change, or only come to visibility (we'll never know which it is). Yet we can never articulate them before the fact: we have to wait for the change. Why was I ready *that afternoon* to put on a pair of old tennis shoes and run around the soccer field on the playing fields across from which we lived until I could run no longer? I can't say. Yet it's one of the defining stories of my life: I got two and a half times around a soccer field before I had to drop to my knees.

But the next day I was out there again, and soon I was running ten times around the whole complex, on the grass around the edge of the woods where the huge metal gas balloons rose and fell over the months, blocking more or less of the sky in their airy cages, painted chalk green against the darker natural green of the woods. And within months I had taken to running more than ten miles, into Washington, down North Capitol Street (in retrospect, somewhat dangerous) to the Capitol, and then back again to the then blue-collar Maryland suburbs of Chillum Heights, where I shared the apartment with my brother.

Pascal

Sometimes the mere suggestion that things should change make us realize they can, and so cause them to do so. Nor should we conclude that we alone hold the key to ourselves: it's not true that others can't change us by force—we might think of Pascal's famous statement that it was enough to kneel down (or be made to kneel?) to be able to pray. If someone had made me run repeatedly, it would have become easier, and I would have ceased dreading it. No one was making me, so I had to wait until the idea occurred to me and I was receptive, a convergence that took its time in coming. How can we plot this convergence more specifically? Certainly we couldn't have plotted it at all if it hadn't happened—we have no way of knowing about all the misses of asteroids in the vastness of space, only the rare impacts.

Even at our most vacuous, we are not zero. Even before we revise our views of ourselves, we are something. Every philosophy, every articulation, presupposes and includes what it diverges from, includes its opposite. This is the pile of books. This point is like Hegel's famous master/slave dialectic: the master needs the slave to be master. The victor needs the vanquished to be victor: from the perspective of the gods, both are equally part of the world; one doesn't replace the other.

When we run, we go into the world of other people—a world that can force us to look for explanations, and frequently does so—and engage in an act "just because." We don't have to run, and yet we do. What we do could be met with a demand for explanation, but isn't usually. In running, taking the life force of movement that we do not control and intensifying it in the world that exists outside of ourselves, we express both sides of this relationship, the subjective and the objective, the self and the world, the explained and the unexplained. In our actions in the world, we are the world that contains all these things, a microcosm of the universe. We exist in a continuous slippage between same and different: five times around, as at the lake, each time different and each time the same—except when it isn't: this is the drama of our Earthly time.

4
Running on the National Mall

When my brother was alive, which is exactly as many years ago as my daughter is old, he lived in a house behind Union Station in Washington. Keith died in February of 1992; Alexandra was born in July. Keith had been ill with the effects of AIDS, off and on, for two years, and toward the end, was pitiful indeed, emaciated and hallucinating. I'm not sure he ever registered that I was to have a daughter, my first child, or that if he did, he cared.

There's not a lot left of my brother in material terms: some photographs in my house, the best of the lot framed and hung on the wall, some diplomas in my mother's house—and odd things like some of his t-shirts from places he'd been that I didn't have the heart to throw out and that now I still sometimes pull from the bottom of my drawer, or a pen I'll grab to write something and remember him holding. And memories, like fragments saved from the wreck. My brother has become a collection of smaller more durable stand-in things, like bits and pieces saved from the wreck, given that the larger, transient entity of the person himself is gone.

The block between his house and the train station used to be a parking lot. I would run across it on my way to the Mall for jogging when I was staying with him, or home from graduate school, or later when I lived back in the area, coming in for the day. This was all before so many things, before my first wife, before my daughter (the marriage, to my childhood sweetheart, was a disaster; the divorce, meant to be a no-fault divorce that would allow us to raise Alexandra amicably, turned into a slug-fest orchestrated by my wife's lawyer; and Alexandra herself turned out to be autistic), before Meg, before Owen and Teddy.

This parking lot, that I had to traverse on my way to the Mall, has long since been taken up by a lofty office building, all glass atrium with trees in the front, the back more forbidding and less transparent up against the quiet residential streets where Keith lived. I'd run up the steps by the much-photographed fountain on Capitol Hill—not photographed so much for its own sake as for that of the U.S. Capitol behind; it's used as the backdrop for a television news program—around the fountain, down the grass in front of the Capitol, by a reflecting pool (in more recent years with water dyed dark to discourage algae, I'd read, as well as to hide the trash that people throw into its shallow waters) and then onto the Mall, after dodging the intermittent traffic on the street in front of the Capitol.

The National Mall is lined with museums, which are one way of preserving the fragments of dead people, bygone eras. My memories of Keith are another way of preserving the past. All of them are versions of the storehouses of small hard things we keep because they are both small and hard: we can't hoard large things, and only the hard things survive. Each of us is like a hamster, or a magpie, with a store of seeds or bright shiny things. The small hard things stand in for much larger chunks of the world: we can't preserve the large things, which usually rot away or are simply incorporated into our ongoing lives, like whole cities we simply build over. So we have our hoards: our museums public or private. It's our way of holding on to the dead.

Only the thing is, it's the way of the living, our way. When we in turn are dead these bits and pieces of the past are re-organized: some are re-classified as junk and thrown away. If anything is saved, it may well be for other reasons than those for which it was saved before: when we're dead, they lose the meaning we assigned to them, and are either thrown away or re-organized by the understanding of other people.

The Bactrian Hoard

In the new National Gallery, I think as I run by this day so many years after Keith's death—I'm visiting a friend and having a run here for old times' sake, so it's inevitable I should think of Keith—is an exhibit from Afghanistan's now-destroyed National Museum (the exhibit catalogue shows it as a bombed-out shell), its treasures now on U.S. exhibit. It seems a win-win situation: the imperial power gets to show off the treasures of its vassal state, for which it shed its blood; the treasures get a home while their building is, at least in theory, being re-built.

The running trails around the Mall, that stretches from the Capitol to the Washington Monument, are packed dirt: really they're not proper running trails at all, but like the bald streaks that quickly make diagonals across squares of college grass by students looking for a shortcut, created by countless feet pounding beside the pavement to avoid the concrete. I've read that the dirt on the National Mall is almost as hard as cement, which is bad for the trees. Still, people are going to run here, and the only other alternative is the sidewalks, which are even harder, not to mention full of tourists.

When I first began running here, in 1974, it was all before jogging became a way of life and a big market niche: this was before running guru Jim Fixx keeled over in mid-stride, before the proliferation of running shoes, before the spin-offs of running togs and exercise fashions.[11] Running was still the province of high school and college athletes, an extension of the "twice around the field" warm-up for the soccer team. Now the waves have washed over and gone: the only people left to run on the Mall are the hairless Marines from 8th and I, who were there before and will be there after, and the newest generation of bright young things who come in the summer to Washington to burnish their resumes and learn the ways of the world.

Today I'm outside, running. Yesterday I was in the museum, looking at the exhibit. We understand running when we think not only about when we run—most typically on the edges of places and times—but also about the times and places where we do not run. We can't run in a building, especially not a museum; the scale isn't right for this kind of motion. We'd bang into things, and break them. It's as if we were to think we could live within one of the miniature rooms, perhaps a two feet across, set into the wall in the Baltimore Museum of Art. We'd break everything just by sticking in our hand. Nor can we peer at the tiny things behind glass when we run, or hanging on the wall in a small room. In a museum, we walk, very slowly. This is the speed for which the building was created. Outside, we run. Running outside a museum makes reference to the two poles of existence: the very quiet and small, and the large and expansive. Running is an action of encompassing: I think of the sensation of running around the grounds of Haverford College, where I had been so unathletic, when I returned there to read from a novel of mine 25 years after I graduated. It was suddenly so small and comprehensible, only a moderate run, perhaps a bit more than 40 min. All of my world that had once seemed so large was held within this span.

The film that accompanies the exhibit inside the museum shows the kind of attitude Americans are trying to foster in Afghanistan. Cosmopolitan curators of the museum hid its treasures from the Taliban (who were busy blowing up a giant Buddha as idolatrous, making sure women were veiled, and reimposing *shari'a*, religious law, among other things) and when the all-clear was given, unpacked them. The film that runs continually in a darkened room in the center of the exhibition—you have to make the decision to bypass it, rather than having to seek it out: everyone enters the back of the projection gallery—shows their wooden boxes, pulled from the darkness of a bank vault, being unpacked. Joy is general: the treasures have survived.

The treasures are of three sorts. The first, and least interesting, are the remnants of a Hellenistic city, of which the Afghans only became aware when the 20th century was well advanced: the King who then ruled the country was visiting a rural area, and was shown a battered Corinthian capital, whose import he understood. Excavations produced some of the usual Hellenistic accouterments of provincial cities, though not numerous and not large: a few roof figures, some carvings, a bronze god or two. They could have come from Alexandria, or Sidon, or anywhere in the Hellenistic world. Because they happened to be on territory now part of the country of Afghanistan, they become Afghani heritage.

The second cache is from the city of Begram. It's a treasure trove of small, expensive objects, such as scholars tell us were the mainstay of traders moving along the connected series of trails from China to the Middle East that are collectively called the Silk Road. The city was already destroyed by the time Marco Polo came through, though there was enough of a collective memory of what had been for the Venetian to write glowingly of what had been, as preserved in the memory of the local people.

These are small hard objects with a vengeance, portable luxury items: concentrated things. Only small, hard, expensive objects, the catalogue tells us, were considered worth the long and arduous trip along the Silk Road, as they could be packed easily, and were worth the barter at the other end. The Begram treasure, at least according to most scholars, is the contents of a store-room of a particularly well-to-do merchant, or perhaps group of merchants. The alternative theory, less accepted nowadays, is that they were a king's store of treasures.

The drinking glasses have proved the most mutable. They've been shattered, but have been once again pieced together around transparent glass cores: they have painted scenes in bright yellows and blues. Molded metal decorations—griffons, lions: handles for pots—fill another shining showcase. But the high point of the Begram treasure are the small, intricately-carved ivory panels of voluptuous women in various poses and surrounded by finely-rendered architectural elements, panels that according to scholars must once have all but covered the wooden chair or throne that has now turned to dust. Only these panels—once you've seen one you never forget the faces and bodies of these people, any more than you can fail to recognize a Benin bronze, once having seen a single panel—have survived, themselves carved from the only part of the elephant to survive: small hard pieces attached to wood that has disintegrated, themselves small and hard enough to be worth the transport from their place of origin and then taken from the opened room at Begram, kept in a museum, then a bank vault, then another museum: these are the small hard things that have survived their civilization. Originally, however, they came from India—yet these too have become Afghani heritage.

The third part of the Afghanistan treasure is the "Bactrian Hoard," the Tillya Tepe treasure, unearthed by chance in Northern Afghanistan after peasants began to talk of a "hill of gold," a hillock nearby where occasionally small bits of gold worked their way to the surface. Soviet archeologists excavated, and discovered what later piecing-together determined was the burial mound of wealthy nomads—who in this case took over a much earlier temple, covered over even in their time—rather than making a mound from scratch, as was their usual practice.

What's on display, and what slumbered in bank vaults in Kabul while the Taliban raged outside—what for that matter had slumbered for almost two millennia before bits and pieces found their way to the surface—is the gold and jewels with which the dead and their burial garments were decorated before being buried. After the excavations were complete, archeologists were able to say that Tillya Tepe was the burial place of a chief, who was placed in the center. Around him were a handful of women, including one called the Princess for her more elaborate funeral accouterments. All were covered with gold and gems.

Thank goodness, I imagine archeologists saying, for the burial practices of the ancients, that took all this lovely jewelry and put it under the surface so that the tides of humanity walking upon the earth, living, dying, revolting, suppressing, moving, and staying put, should have no effect on it: not melting it down, not breaking or stealing it, not pulling it from its (to archeologists) all-important context (oh how archeologists love the dead: they make things stand still), but instead irrelevant to it, so that millennia later they can be displayed for the edification of the imperial power of a later age.

Nowadays we take off all of the jewelry of the dead but wedding rings without precious stones—and usually not even those go into the grave. We're not about to make the mistake of the Pharaohs, whose graves were usually robbed within a few short years of their being put in them: they went to their graves with too much stuff. Thus we will provide poor pickings for the archeologists of the year 4,000—assuming anyone is around. Still, like the Pharaohs, we Americans pump our dead full of preservatives that may well help their bodies resist the worms for some decades: the illusion we're after here is what the Egyptians in fact achieved, the preservation of the body. Too bad nobody could tell them that the bodies would survive, but be reduced to the leering leathery statues of unwrapped mummies, the organs dessicated to smears in their Canopic jars. Who would want to reinhabit a dried smear?

Cemetery

Graves are one way we make small hard things that replace the dead, such as the grave if the Bactrian Hoard. Only they turn out not to be as permanent as we think they are. I watched the day Keith's grave was moved: my mother clearly needed some emotional support, and asked that I come. I didn't run that day either: under some circumstances and in some places we simply don't.

She had chosen his first site because it was on the shores of a lake. Then one day she came to find that the plot between Keith (if he could still be so referred to) and the lake had been not only sold, but filled, and not just with another grave and its normally sized headstone, but with a large mausoleum. My mother was livid. She had understood that nothing would come there and now Keith's view, if that's what it was, of the lake was occluded by this dastardly family's monument. She knew the family this belonged to, and held them responsible. She complained to the funeral director of the place that controlled the cemetery, but after apologizing, he had said he could do nothing. They owned the spot, and could build there what they wanted.

My mother generally gets her own way. In this case, she had Keith's grave moved to closer to the water, just across the path: here, the funeral director assured her, there couldn't possibly be graves between Keith and the lake because of the drop-off: the land became too unstable for graves. (On some river banks or in coastal areas the graves simply wash away, so I hope the funeral director had this drop-off correctly calculated.) The transfer was a surprisingly simple process for something we conceive of as eternal. A backhoe scraped away the thin skin of dirt on the concrete box; a crane attached to a truck lifted it up by its built-in handles (the same that were used to lower it into the first hole). It was loaded on a truck for the twenty or thirty yards away, lowered into the new hole, already dug, and the job was done.

We think of interment as committing to the earth, but it isn't really. It's temporary placement. The dirt can simply be scraped away, and new grass simply laid down. Even deeper graves are plundered all the time: their contents to end in museums—and the dead themselves are not considered off limits, in the case of the Egyptians or these Bactrian nomads, so completely has their world disappeared, turned to its small hard things of preserved bodies, their casings, jewelry, statues of gods and goddesses, and accompanying mummified animals. Virtually all of these things have now been dug up from graves and put in museums.

Museums

When, occasionally in a catalogue of antiques for sale, one sees something described as "museum-quality," this means that it's so good it's worthy of a museum: museums are the *crème de la crème*, the small hard things of the small hard things. Comparably, in developing nations, first class is sometimes indicated by calling a product—beer, perhaps—"export quality": so good it's worthy to be exported, yet here you are in, say, Bombay (Mumbai), drinking it. It's worthy of a museum, but you can buy it and show it in your own home!

Museums contain what we are supposed to save first in case of fire—a fire in our civilization, perhaps, as the Taliban represented for the cosmopolitan museum heads of the National Museum of Afghanistan, protecting the Bactrian Hoard in the bank vault. But this means that we have to throw away the soft parts that surrounded them, at least what to us seems the soft part—which may not be what seemed so to them. Soft is relative to hard, and hard is defined by the perceiver. The person dies; the flesh is the first to go, then the bones, which for some intermediate periods serve as the hard dry things: bundles of bones are put into reliquary boxes among the Fang, and guardians perched on top of them; the bones and skulls of monks are used for decoration in some monasteries in Italy and Iberia.

The act of mummification was the Egyptian attempt to turn the body itself into a small hard thing: it dried up, and its organs were removed, but there it all was, as the soul, the "ka," would need it in the afterlife. We might say that a dried organless shell is of no interest for the afterlife, but the Egyptians saw things differently. So there's nothing logical or self-evident about what constitutes a small hard thing, or the form it takes: we just have to decide what we'll accept as a stand-in for the thing that's now gone. In Chinese graves, we read, gradually clay statues of people supplanted the slaughtered servants of earlier times; in the Grecian-influenced period in Egypt, masks of the deceased, necessary for the "ka" to recognize its body, were replaced by wax portraits of the person inside, made during life and (scholars think) probably hung in their houses until needed on mummy bundles. Only the people themselves could say what was necessary to constitute a small hard thing: for some, the two-dimensional image in wax, for some the dead body of a servant, for some a clay statue.

On Italian and southern French graves, portraits of the dead in frames are set on flat above-ground graves as a way of preserving the now-rotted appearance of the face. They are part of the small hard things that are preserved. While on the grave they relate to the vanished person, but the day may come when they don't: they're removed from their graves, or the graves themselves cease to exist. At this point their relation as small hard things is no longer to individuals, but to a time and place more generally. The day may come when they fill museums, as indeed the dismembered monuments of Père-Lachaise in Paris may some day fill the museums of the fourth millennium. They're still be small hard things, but not (as they now still are) of individual people's lives, rather of the times in which they lived. Probably there will be so many of them that we'll be able to be picky about artistic quality: it won't be a picture of Grandma, it'll be a picture of a woman, of better or lesser quality.

This is the way we further choose among small hard things for the socially defined collections of small hard things we call museums. Museums are to a society as Nona's portrait on a grave is to her. Art history reduces the individual church's Virgin and Child to examples of a style, and these are ranked by other criteria entirely than those which decided that they would fill the space over the altar of the Chiesa di Santa X. Thus there's nothing illegitimate about the way art museums take African masks out of the context that bound them to their villages, or their people, or their ceremony, and organize them by other principles—though this is a frequent claim. That's just what we do to turn them into small hard things for larger groups. This is not a fact of Western vs. non-Western. We do it with our own art, though of course not as thoroughly: it's our own art, after all, and we remember more particular things about it that seem to be part of it. But art exposition as an undertaking is based on making small hard things out of small hard things: we can't retain all the paintings and masks ever made, or put them on show.

The John Howard MacFadden collection in the Philadelphia Museum of Art consists of dozens of Romneys, Gainesboroughs, and Raeburns, all stripped of the context of the individual country houses in which they once hung as the portraits of specific people, Grandma, or Great Grandma, or Uncle Henry. The rooms, dark paneling mostly, in which they hang in the never-land of the museum in Philadelphia, are taken from specific houses, now largely destroyed: photographs for consultation show us what they looked like. But nobody cares, except as an afterthought or a scholarly footnote. In the museum, they are portraits in a generic English Country House. The Indian temple in the same museum is the amalgam of several temples, with statues from various other places; in the Cloisters in New York, elements from three different cloisters are combined to produce a peaceful, fountain-platsching whole here in New York city, which never had a real Medieval cloister.

Museums are thus the places we construct to hold the smallest and hardest things chosen from many small hard things, themselves chosen from among countless large soft things that do not get preserved or put on view. That this is not a final action, and remains a specific one, is seen from the fact that we can run outside the museum: the more concentrated we make the small hard things we enshrine, the more free we are to move faster than any speed appropriate to them in other places. Condensation into small hard things doesn't change the world; it just frees up spaces to be used for completely other things.

In the same way, solving a problem doesn't change the world, it merely re-orders it: the smaller and harder it is, the tighter-knit, the more the rest of the world is liberated to be used for other things. Thus one person can't save others time, or trouble, or psychic energy by re-vamping the world forever: the re-vamping changes the world, so that the other person now deals with a world in which what the other person made is a fact. But it's a fact surrounded by the world of the new person, which is larger than this fact, larger than anything precise that it inherits. We only coalesce our own reality into small hard things; what we forget sometimes is that someone else starting with the small hard thing that had to be coalesced from our world at such a price faces a different world than the one from which it was necessary for us to coalesce it. Thus we never hand things on; all we do is change the world. Why bother, we might wonder? The more efficiently we set up museums in specific places with all the small hard things together, the easier it is to avoid them altogether and have a nice run outdoors instead.

Personal museums

In the same way that museums and the very rich get the pick of the world historical lot—the best Greek vases, the best T'ang grave statues—each of us individually hoards small hard things that stand in for much more. All of us make personal museums; museums are the museums of museums. A person we knew may be long dead, but we keep a photograph on the mantel. This is our shrine to the dead that allows us to go about our business. We frame our college diploma, representing so much work: that done, we go on to other things than college. We put on our mantel the glass vase we bought in Venice. We can't bring back Venice, but here's the object we bought there. Nor do we make personal museums only of tangible things. An experience may have been excruciating, but we tell ourselves that what we got from it was the following lesson: this is what we learned, its fruit, the flower of the plant.

We set up situations that produce small hard things and acknowledge them: birthdays, graduations, weddings. The pieces of paper that stand for them are made harder by being put behind glass, or on a pedestal. All our lives are the process of separating the wheat from the chaff, given that we cannot keep the chaff. And this is circular: the wheat is what we can keep, the chaff, what we cannot. If we get so much wheat we're overwhelmed, we change the sorting technique, and save not all the wheat but instead, only the perfectly shaped wheat, or the roundest (or for that matter squarest) wheat, or the whitest (or darkest) kernels. (Black pearls are so expensive because most pearls are white.) The irregular ones become filed with the chaff: we let these go.

There can be conflict between the personal museums we all make and the public ones. It's rare when someone's personal collection can be translated without further sorting to a public museum: when this is possible it's usually been acquired with a view to this: only those objects acquired which would translate directly to a public museum, where things are interesting even to people with no personal connection to them. Very few people's collections (photos, diplomas) would be of general interest.

Sometimes rich people set up the contents of their houses as museums: something, an object, may have meant a good deal to an individual, but it's only rarely when his or her "house museum" turns out to be of general interest—or if it does, becomes interesting only as a slice of life, a time period preserved, not a museum of individually interesting objects. The Krieger Museum in Washington would have been a stunning place to be invited to dinner—a house by Philip Johnson, with Monets on the walls—far beyond the interest level of most houses and most personal art collections. But as a Washington museum on the same list with the Phillips, it's a failure: the house as its own end is not worth the trip or the admission fee, and the paintings are like paler versions of things one can see for free in the National Gallery. Nor is there any apparent reason for these paintings to be in this house: it would have been far better for the house to be inhabited by other people after the Kriegers' deaths, and the paintings dispersed. By contrast, the museum of James Brady in Cuernavaca, though containing few individually interesting works—some Narayit pre-Columbian pottery, a Frieda Khalo—makes a far greater impression. Filled with colorful junk and open to the semi-tropical air, it seems its own world.

Keith is now his diplomas, images of him when alive, and a gravestone. But every household has its cache of diplomas: they're only meaningful for a generation or two, and then perhaps as "antiques," stripped of personal connections. One day in an "antiques" shop in Lancaster County, Pennsylvania, a German-language marriage certificate was presented for my inspection, with the hope I'd buy it. It was an engraving, that had been personalized with handwritten names, and tinted with watercolors. I refused it: I could read it, and so it seemed still the marriage certificate of real people, if dead ones. Why would I want it in my house? I had no connection with them. Given someone who couldn't read it, or the passage of time, or a museum with a great number of them so that they became only their formal qualities, and it might become a publicly accessible small, hard thing. As it was, it drifted uncomfortably between the personal and the general, in the process of being reorganized as another kind of small hard thing.

Colonel

Keith isn't the only one who's gone. My father too is reduced to only a few small hard things: diplomas, some photographs, a silver napkin ring he used in his college dining hall (!), his Army name plate with Colonel's insignia, the flag, folded into a triangle, that briefly lay on his coffin. To be sure, I treasure virtually nothing about my father, so I am not eager to keep memories, or memorabilia. But I at least have the choice how much to keep, or how little: nobody else cares. My brother is dead and my mother can't speak of my father without bitterness.

My paternal grandmother is even less: for my purposes, she is some fading memories, her teaching certificate from 1901 (the form was from the nineteenth rather than the then-new twentieth century, and clearly they either hadn't gotten new forms or had decided to use up the old, so the printed letters said 18__ and had been crossed out), her school bell, and a teaching certificate. On the certificate are numbers, the scores she'd gotten on teaching examinations. The certificate itself is a "II Class" certificate: from this distance the meaning of either the scores or the "II" would have been gone, washed out as some of the many soft things that turn to dust. Except that my grandmother had given me the form that served as an addendum, filled out in spidery handwriting: a letter from a year later with new, higher scores, and the notation that if she sent back the "II Class" certificate, she would be entitled to a "I Class" one. She didn't know why I wanted this certificate (this is 45 years ago), was reluctant to give it to me, and parted with it only if I promised to add the letter and the explanation that this was only the provisional certificate. So her sense of shame and inadequacy has by chance survived the rotting away, at least so long as I remember it: it's now part of the small hard thing of the certificate.

Keith isn't just his diplomas and the framed pictures. Occasionally I'll come on some candid snapshots of him, which are perhaps more revealing, but also less attractive than the good ones I have framed. These "ready-for-prime-time" ones have become Keith, the way movie stars, say Gary Cooper with his hands in his pockets, or Marilyn Monroe with her skirt up above her knees, become the one over-reproduced photograph we associate with them. Save for these things, my brother has turned to dust. Certainly nothing of his emotions remains, just the outlines of his life told in the way that we construct the soft hard things of biographies. Had a Ph.D. in musicology from Catholic University, played the 'cello for many years in the Kennedy Center Opera House orchestra, died of AIDS at age 40.

"What a waste," my mother said bitterly one day. It was the most negative thing I've ever heard her say, and uncharacteristic. It made me wonder if that's what she'd been thinking all along. Otherwise she says nothing, or treats Keith's early death as merely part of life. She changes the artificial flowers on his grave, now moved from behind the offending mausoleum, with the seasons: her garage has a pile of the plastic and silk flowers that rotate and presumably are thrown out when they become weather-beaten.

Silk flowers

Artificial flowers too, such as those my mother puts on Keith's grave, are to the more fragile real ones as diplomas and the few best photographs are to a person's life. They freeze the blur of motion, and in freezing, produce another sort of product, the way jams are never are the same as the fresh fruit, or pickles the same as the cucumbers from which they were made. When I was young I took a brief sideline from building models and constructing a fishpond into drying flowers. Sand laced with silica is the necessary material, and some flowers dry more successfully than others. This wasn't the only way I tried to make small hard things of flowers. In a spate of candle-making, I tried dipping the fragile white flowers of the hedge in wax to see if I could preserve them. I think they rotted inside of their waxen mummy cases and were thrown away: the experiment wasn't a success.

All these were attempts to make small hard things, longer-lasting flowers out of shorter-lasting. What's achieved is by contrast the immutable. But of course it's only relative immutability. We seek longer-lasting versions of what we know to be shorter-lived, but they're still not very long-lived in absolute terms: they only seem so by contrast. Dried flowers fall prey to jostling, and dust, and years of handling by careless housecleaners—unless, of course, they are made even smaller and harder by being enclosed in glass away from the dust and the housemaids. Yet glass can be broken: in terms of centuries it's one of the softer of the small hard things. The plastic and silk flowers my mother puts on my brother's grave ultimately fade, or simply shred with too much weather.

So too the headstones of graves, that we construct of stone because that seems to us to be immutable. For those people without access to stones, wood has to do, as in the famous carved grave posts of Madagascar. These last for longer than a few years only if they're rooted up and put in climate-controlled Western museums. Still, wood is more immutable than nothing at all, or flowers—though all longevity is relative. Plants are more immutable than their flowers, especially annuals; trees more than plants. Yet trees too are struck by lightning, and have natural lives measured in hundreds of years—except the remote 4,000 year old bristlecone pines of the Owens Valley in the Eastern Sierra. And these have only survived so long because they were so remote, and so scrubby.

No artificial flower survives as long as bristlecone pines: so why do we bother? But of course the lives of artificial flowers aren't measured in terms of those of bristlecone pines, but only in terms of what they're compared with: real flowers. Real flowers, in their turn, last longer than evanescent lighting effects of sun on clouds, or on water: we don't capture these by making artificial clouds, but by painting, or admiring Impressionist paintings that hold these for as long as the canvases are protected from their own natural degradation. Yet wars burn canvases. I have a book called *Lost Treasures of Europe*: the fatalities of World War II, paintings that no longer exist, buildings in rubble (as most of Dresden remained for many years).[12] What remains of most of these now lost artworks is photographs, whose reproducibility, and relative lack of value, has made them survive; for other lost artworks we have fragments or references: classics scholars try to reconstruct the basics of lost plays by the dramatists from citations in other works.

We construct graves with harder memorials—stone, or wood if that's all we have—because they seem long-lasting. But of course vandals can break even headstones, and do. The concrete vault that made the process of moving my brother from one plot to another so humdrum is unaffected by the passage of a few decades. In a few hundred years, however, it's liable to have developed cracks. Saints' bodies are all the time producing miracles in that they remained incorruptible (as we say) in the grave for centuries, like that of St. Francis Xavier, in Goa: we're not surprised that a Roman coin from much longer ago has remained "incorruptible" (we wouldn't even say this) for much longer. People spend great amounts of money for "antiques" a hundred years old, but they have only to bend down and pick up rocks that are as old as the Earth itself.

Ozymandias
The Romantics made much of the evanescence of all things: think of Ozymandias' statue in Shelley's famous eponymous sonnet, bidding (so the narrator and perhaps the poet imagined) the viewer of the statue, the hearer of the story or reader of the poem, to "look on my works, ye mighty, and be afraid." All passes: it's the source of the Romantic melancholy. But this is only half the story, the fact that a small hard thing is typically less small and hard than another thing. The other half, the positive half, is that small hard things are in fact smaller and harder than what they're more usually compared with, as plastic flowers easily outlast real ones. Small hard things are no more defeats than they are victories: the Romantics saw only part of the story.

Small hard things only gain value because they contrast with something that's gone. The museum, that storehouse of small hard things, needs the world outside in which I run. We're impressed by having Grandma's diamond ring because Grandma is very old, or dead: yet the stone has been around, in one form or another, since it was formed in the ground, and so is the same no matter who owned it, or when it was pulled from the ground and cut. Matter, in some form, has been around since matter was created, but that fact doesn't make it valuable to us. We're not impressed by the incorruptibility of plastic, so long as we think of it as plastic: we just don't see it change. But a plastic X, where X is otherwise transitory, can impress us. And we like things made from the semi-living substance of bone and ivory because the animal—elephant, walrus—has itself rotted away.

Horreur des Revenants

In running on the National Mall, about opposite the Natural History Museum, I've seen a cluster of people over under the trees: there are families on the grass, and tourists sitting on the benches. I notice them because the man could be Keith, at least from the back. I'm not close enough to confirm it isn't Keith, dead for almost two decades, but I know it isn't. Nor would I want it to be. We can't save all of life; we only save small hard bits of it. We save the small hard bits of memories and things because the large soft parts are gone. Having the dead return would require the complete reorganization of our lives.

Keith lived to see nothing past the fact that Alexandra was coming: not her birth, not my subsequent divorce from her mother, not the discovery of her autism, not my second marriage, not his two little nephews with Meg. If, therefore, it were to be him on the other side of the Mall (let's say he really died, but now is back), I'd have to begin by bringing him up to speed with all that had happened. The same is true if I were to meet him in heaven (let's say the most literal and touching interpretations of the afterlife turn out to be true). Our first conversation will be a long one. Nor is my life over; I'm sure there will be more before I'm allowed to ascend the golden staircase, if I do. Or do those in heaven, perhaps looking down from the clouds, somehow know what happens to the ones close to them down below?

It seems unlikely that they'd care. One day, I watched my mother, on the porch of her Adirondack house, try to stand up a wooden drying rack. It had been folded up so it was flat, albeit thick. She tried once to lean it up against the screening, strengthened with vertical wooden struts. The base was too close to the wall, and it fell over. She tried again, pulling the base further away from the wall (she wanted it to take up as little room as possible). It wavered, but ultimately fell over. She tried a third time, pulling the base away from the screening even further. This time was a charm: this was the ideal positioning, far enough from the wall to stand up, close enough not to be too much of an impediment to people walking by.

Knowing that you have to pull out the base of something you want to lean is knowledge that seems peculiarly Earthbound. I don't know why the Blessed should have to know about such things. So it seems likely that knowledge like this, so hard-won on Earth, will simply wash away, along with all the other situational knowledge so important to our temporal lives: how fast you can run without winding yourself, how long to leave the fried egg before flipping it, what clothes to wear to what kind of function, how hot the temperature has to be before a beer tastes fabulous, what shirt goes with this tie. None of this knowledge, it seems, will survive death. Yet this is the knowledge that makes us who we are.

If all this is gone, as it seems likely to be in any other realm but this one, in which it makes sense, then it's unclear how individual angels, or souls, can be any different from each other. I can start by realizing that Keith probably wouldn't even care to hear the things I'd have to tell him. But, for that matter, what would make him Keith rather than Joe Schmoe? Or distinguish either from Jane Doe? If it's true that in Heaven all such details blank out, or wash away, then why would I have a closer relationship with the detail-less blank that used to be my brother than with any of the other detail-less blanks populating Heaven's realm? If my own tastes and proclivities—Schubert and Bartók, chardonnay, and the well-turned phrase—are also leeched out of my soul in leaving my body behind, how am I different at all from all the other similarly purified entities drifting (for surely disembodied spirits don't walk, which presupposes friction with the ground) about me?

Many funeral services contain a promise that we'll see our loved ones in the Beyond. But if we do, we'll either be so out of sync with them, or so in sync we won't have anything to talk about with them—assuming the Blessed (or any other Afterlife denizens) talk, moving air over the larynxes they've left behind, or perhaps thought-communicate, which presupposes synapses firing in a brain they wouldn't have.

Ice man

The few times it seems the dead do come back are in fact deeply upsetting. It turns out we don't actually want it to happen even if we say we do, which is why we hold on to small hard things instead: they are part of our lives in the here and now. We don't want the past, we want the small hard things that stand for it.

A European legend re-told in many versions tells of the young husband, or in some versions wooer and gallant, the rustic Romeo (the story requires the Alps or the Carapathians, central or Eastern Europe, so he's imagined in Lederhosen and a Loden cap with a feather) who goes up into the mountains to hunt and is never heard of again. The young wife, or sweetheart, looks every day for him to return. Her hope, like new wine turning to vinegar, day by day grows more and more bitter, and finally she is certain he is dead. After a decent interval the church bells peal his passing in the village in the valley, and after however many years of fighting or acceptance, the now no longer so young woman marries another, or marries again. She lives her life, her children by this other man grow up; her hair whitens, her back begins to hunch, her skin grows flaccid and her face becomes that of a crone. And yet she never forgets her first love, who vanished up into the mountains and was never heard of again.

Then one day some of the young men of the village—younger than her own sons—come down from the snows. They have the deer they've shot. And they've found, coughed up from an avalanche, or the shift of a glacier, the body of a man as young as they—at least in appearance. He is frozen stiff, but still in the full bloom of youth, his muscles strong, his hair gold, his skin taut. And quite dead.

The body is brought into the village; the old woman, along with all the other villagers comes to see where they've laid him out in the village square. She jostles forward in the crowd, grows closer, is at the front of the buzzing throng—then suddenly she puts a hand to her heart and falls onto the cobblestones in a faint: it's her lover from so long ago, lost in the mountains, preserved in the youth she has long ago left behind—a man younger than her children's children.

So it seems Keith would be to me, separated by the passage of time and all that has happened—though now the distance between us in years is not so great as between the young lovers of the story. If he stood before me now, in fact, the man of almost two decades ago, it's not clear that the living one, me, would seem older: at his death he'd lost most of his hair, naturally—to pass over the effects of the illness that turned him into a bedridden muscle-less old man in his last months—and this was gray. I would possibly still seem the younger, as I was in life. Still, I've lived a long time beyond him: Keith died when he was 40. I haven't been 40 for a long time, and my second marriage and my children all come after that: now I am the older. I've seen things he never saw: my own family, of course, but the politics of the last two decades, the Internet, and global warming. Some day my own children, now young boys, will say the same of me. Poor Dad, he never saw X and Y, not to mention Z, all things they will take so for granted. What, if I meet them in Heaven, will we have to talk about?

The time line goes in one direction only, and it can't, it seem, have loops. It's better that the dead stay dead, not be disgorged from glaciers, or met up with a half century later in some other form: why else do we have such a horror of ghosts, imagined as those come back from the dead? They should be content with the finality of who they were, not try to be like us. After all, we've already saved them: in the small hard things they leave behind, things that can be transported along the Silk Road—and in our memories, the small hard things of our minds. We don't need them; we have our mementoes. The only kind of transcendence we achieve is as part of the here and now—which is why we run.

War and Peace

Art history is a way of re-organizing personal mementoes into a more general way of preserving the past. The individual artwork preserves the past too, only entities more general than individuals: thus each one re-organizes the past into small hard things, and is in turn reorganized. Fiction is a way of preserving not individuals but ways of doing things, time periods: individuals as typical, or atypical, the way the Costume Institutes of museums put out dresses of the 18th century not as those of individual people, but as "morning dress of an aristocratic Frenchwoman, 1730s"—or Gainsborough portraits not as pictures of Great-Grandma but pictures by Gainsborough.

Memories of the dead are what's left when they're gone; novels and representations of people who never were is the way we preserve more general entities: a time, a way of life. All are the tips of icebergs: the tip stands in for a vast amount that we can never get back. They are the small hard things that we hold onto because we cannot have the large soft ones any more. If ever we could have the large soft ones again—the people now dead, the time period—these crystallizations would lose their point. Fiction is pointless if we compare it to real people—which is Plato's conviction that poets lie, echoed by John Searle's more contemporary assertion that fiction makes statements with the form but not the content of assertions.[13] What both Plato and Searle fail to see is that fiction doesn't serve as the small hard thing with respect to real people, but with something more general: a way of doing things. If we lived among these fictional people, we wouldn't need the fiction: we'd preserve them in different ways.

Aristotle, in his *Poetics*, held that the essence of art was imitation. But Aristotle was wrong. It's not imitation we're engaged in when we have imaginary people say things on a stage: it's the construction of a small hard thing that will outlive people. It's by contrast with real people that we don't have access to that this seems solid, worth looking at; the process of making something small and hard frequently involves transforming it, like drying the flowers, or making others in silk and plastic. It's no more imitation to have the words of people who never were than it is to make glass or silk flowers: we're not primarily imitating flowers, we're rendering them less transitory—the imitation is what makes the less transitory versions of the more, the link. Aristotle focused on the sameness; but it makes more sense to focus on the difference. Only the difference explains why we'd make them at all.

The tragedies of Sophocles don't, most essentially, imitate people's words, they render them less transitory, because written and spoken again, not to mention more intense. The photograph of my dead brother isn't most essentially an imitation, it's a form of his life that's longer-lasting than he himself: to make it longer lasting still, we put it behind glass and hang it out of harm's way on the wall. An obituary isn't an imitation of a life; it's a form that's small and hard. A narration in words of feelings isn't an imitation; it's a more permanent version, relatively speaking.

A new translation of *War and Peace*, that retains the original French of this francophone Russian aristocracy of the time of Napoleon, echoes and exemplifies the fact that the dead need to stay dead: they've become irrelevant in any case, having been replaced by the small hard things that survive them. Tolstoy has a guest speaking of ghosts at the *soirée* which opens the book. He calls them *revenants*—"*j'ai horreur des histories des revenants*," he says. It's old-fashioned French, certainly for now and perhaps even for then (the Russian aristocracy spoke a proudly 18th century French in these turbulent years after the French Revolution, the king barely dead, Napoleon usurping the throne—and subsequently invading Moscow): *revenants* for ghosts, where now we would say *fantômes*, phantoms: *revenants*, those who return. It seems vaguely Shakespearean, since Shakespeare has Hamlet speak of death as the "undiscovered country from whose bourn no traveller e'er returns"—though puzzlingly enough, the ghost of Hamlet's father, only a few lines later, seems to have done just that, and indeed does so repeatedly in the course of the play.

These Russian aristocrats, for instance: how alluring they are through their one-way mirror of the novel, and how much at a loss we'd be to deal with them if suddenly the time line were folded and these two points of our present and their past, separated by centuries, were to touch. Luckily, we'd be able to speak to them in French: few of us speak Russian. But our French would be odd to them, as a Montreal friend of mine smiled tolerantly one day at my "Parisian slang"—for me it was just French. We'd have to explain cars, now apparently in the process themselves of becoming old-fashioned, and telephones, and electricity. They'd understand America, which existed even then as a place of refuge: but how to explain that it's no longer an agrarian nation of simple farmers, but an urban agglomeration, the "*hyper-puissance*" (sole super-power, at least until China finally rises) and is old enough for the urban meccas to have gotten dingy and dilapidated? That all of Jules Verne's world has come true, the flying machines, the submarines—though we'd have to explain Jules Verne as well: how to explain Jules Verne to a world whose literature ended with Byron?

In Hollywood movies of time travel, the premise is always that those from a different—which is to say, inferior—time, joyfully embrace the conveniences of our world, recognizing Progress as such and bowing in feverish subservience to us. But who says that in reality those from another time would be so eager to become us? What if they instead tried to make us like them? It's not irrelevant that such movies are made for us, not them. (The premise that we are the measure of all things is also what changes the characters in the Disney movie *Aladdin*, a Hollywood cartoon version of a story set in the Baghdad of *1001 Nights* into wise-cracking American teen-agers, and has the genie do riffs that are only comprehensible to someone of our moment, not its.[14]) If everything revolves around us, we will set to educating the heathen with a will. But what if, puzzlingly, they don't want to be educated? What if, worse, we discover that the task of educating them is simply too large? How to talk to the dead? The challenge is simply too big. Instead, we replace the dead by small hard things, and individuals by the general of a Costume Institute or a novel.

The world of a novel saves the past, but not so individually as a portrait of Grandma—it's saved more at the level of a Gainsborough, or an "English Country House, ca 1730." The characters of a novel are like fish in an aquarium: the unit is the aquarium, it's not about the individual fish. And like fish in an aquarium, the characters in a novel can't get out: we can put our face right up to the glass, but we cannot enter their world. They take for granted the things they take for granted, we ours, and the two never meet: we note the difference of their world as givens, and understand the things that we have in common.

For example we note the extreme beauty of the Princess Hélène in the first scene of *War and Peace*, re-arranging the folds of her dress and the diamond necklace around her graceful neck; the response of her brother—people can't decide whether it's extremely clever or extremely stupid (he's the one who doesn't like ghost stories); the mother asking for a favor for her son; the man of whom the favor is asked who at first resists and then gives in. This is what we can understand of these people of whom we fail to understand so much: more troublingly, these are people even more illusory than the dead, people who never existed. How would we react if they came alive into our own time? (Woody

Allen imagines Emma Bovary transplanted to New York, after the hero of his story "The Kugelmass Episode" visits her in her world, on a page of her novel: she becomes very 70s and New York: neurotic, whiney, wanting to "take classes" and go shopping.[15])

We'd react badly. So we go to museums, read *War and Peace*, go for runs, and demand that the dead stay dead. After all, that's what it means to be dead.

I.M. Pei

The new National Gallery—as I still think of it—fills the triangle closest to the Mall and is the building with the Bactrian Hoard. Now I'm on my second loop, and run by it again.

Nothing has changed in the meantime, I'd say, but that's only because I'm focusing on the fact that the building hasn't fallen down: certainly the trees aren't exactly the same, the cars in front of it have changed, and the people on its steps are different.

It's a sharp-edged I.M. Pei building, embracing the triangle-ness of the lot it's built on rather than denying it. The sharpest edge has, over the years—Keith never lived to see this either—been darkened in an uneven stain by thousands of tourist hands, trying to see just how sharp it is (not sharp enough to cut flesh). The Mall itself is a great emptiness, like the central bubble between all this line-up of museums tucked into its sides. You enter the central space: green, marked by impromptu playing fields, and on the side, trees—and then pick a side to enter. The New National Gallery mimics this central void with things tucked into corners—and the old does so as well. Yet the two buildings are contraries. The old National Gallery is a welling up; the new is a damping down. The older building, a neo-classical John Russell Pope conception, has a central rotunda inspired by the Pantheon in Rome, with a round colonnade and a huge marble fountain surmounted by the Giambologna "Mercury" that's come to be the synecdoche of the building, being reproduced on the flags that hang in front of it at Tourmobile stops, placed along the gravel path along which I run. The ceiling seems to rise up, and the fountain with its statue: Mercury with winged feet, the caduceus in his hand and a winged helmet that pulls the visitor's eye up into the ceiling. The paintings are not only off to the side of this central bubble, but off the sides of the sides: each of the two wings—one that starts with Giotto and moves around to Rembrandt, the other of which starts with Goya and Constable and moves around to the Impressionists—has itself a central core of emptiness rising to vaults, the eyes drawn up by the pedestals of the life-sized statues which are white marble in one wing, dark bronze in another: the paintings, ostensibly the purpose of this building, are tucked into the galleries on the side.

In the bonier, sharp-edged shape of the triangular new building, the central space seems an exhalation, not an inhalation: a void from which stick out the sharp elbows of the corner exhibition rooms. And the equivalent of the Mercury for the new National Gallery doesn't rise from the floor, it hangs down from the ceiling, weighing down the space: Calder's huge red mobile, which appears on the Tourmobile signs for the new National Gallery. Its most grateful vistas are not those of the person entering its doors—even here you don't enter directly into the space, but into a shadowed underhang of a balcony that seems like the shaded ramps leading out to a sun-struck bullring—but from a balcony or two up, the staircases up the side by the Matisse tower (the museum's most intimate space, along with the curving staircases that lead up the sides and are planted with bromeliads set in stones and drawing light from above) that allow the viewer to lean on a balcony edge and look over at the complex arrangement of light and shadow, walkway with people, stairs, moving and not, people emerging underneath the overhang below into the space dotted by potted trees, the mobile at eye level and drifting in great heavy counterclockwise sweeps (not a motor, I've read, but the natural effect of air currents that send spinning even something that weighs tons), no longer hanging menacingly overhead but as if one were in an airplane contemplating the clouds outside the window.

I was in one of these spiral staircases yesterday, my face pressed to the glass cases in which the Bactrian Hoard glows. I wasn't alone: the rooms were dotted with the darkened shapes of viewers, all shadowy in rooms in which the most striking thing is the glowing scatter of gold lit by unseen spotlights in the center.

Gold

People have always been fascinated by gold precisely for its quality of incorruptibility. Silver is similarly shiny, but it tarnishes: the gold death mask of Tutankhamun still gleams as if newly-made, but silver jewelry of the same time is usually turned to black corruption. So these people were buried with things that already were the small hard things of their time, which is to say valuable: as valuable as the small, compact carved miniatures from the hard part of the elephant that survive today and that provided the reason for the trade along the Silk Road. This is the nature of value: the small and hard. The person passes away, leaving memories; the body decays, leaving only gold jewelry. The value is with respect to what it stands in for.

Photographs taken of the graves when opened are displayed along with the gold hoard: the collapsed skull of one of the women and the pile of dust that was her body still retains the gold shapes once sewn into her robes in the pattern they held on the long-gone cloth. Still, not l00% of the bodies are gone—but what survives isn't a part that probably would have interested anyone: we tend to focus on head and front. No, it's the back skin of the "prince," pushed into the sand, that has been preserved—cloth fragments and all. From this, archeologists have been able to reconstruct the embroidery and cut of the robes; drawings on the walls derived from the position of the gold pieces in the dust show what these people would have worn in death.

Nor is the Bactrian Hoard merely dozens of tiny golden stars or circles sewn in patterns on disintegrated clothing. There are daggers that lay in the tombs by the disintegrating hands of the dead, bracelets that encircled dead wrists, brooches, and even a portable crown of thin gold leaves that could be taken apart and put back together, like an artificial Christmas tree where the buyer has to insert the branches into the core of a trunk.

The workmanship is amazing: bits of turquoise contrast with the gold, making Earth spirits and various heavenly beings (the catalogue points out how surprisingly cosmopolitan these nomads were: the inspiration for the designs comes from lands far away, India or Persia). Now they're removed from their dust, the darkness of their hill, and entombed in glass cases shimmering with light. And they're gorgeous—as beautiful as the day they were made—so we assume, as we see no deterioration. More so, in fact: we see them in a way that no one ever saw them in the time from which they came, much as we see the pediments of the Parthenon up close and personal, as no worshipper in the temple after Phidias had done his work could have seen them, far above and shrouded in shadow as they would have been. These objects weren't meant to be looked at, but to be buried with individuals. To us the individuals are meaningless, but the time period—so far away from us—everything. So these objects are small hard things, only of other icebergs than those they were intended as—tips of other worlds. We're re-assigned them as ways to preserve the past.

But to be shown in an art museum, they can't just be representative of their time: other museums show shelves of pottery shards of interest only to the most dedicated of history lovers. These objects are not only made of a precious substance and fragments of their time; in addition they're beautiful, using the material as an important aspect of the object in a way that only completely successful works of art do—which is why we can show them in an art museum. In curios, a lesser form of carving, the material is incidental, or secondary. Thousands of over-meticulous Chinese ivory carvings of boats and goddesses use the carvability of the medium to achieve detail, but the whiteness and shininess of the medium are incidental to the product, as is the shape of the tusk. And hundreds of bad African ivory carvings are too beholden to the curving shape of the tusk that seems to constrain the figures within. All too frequently, Chinese ivory carving obliterates the medium, African is bound by it. A tusk, at least in its central part where there is some thickness and the top has begun to thin a bit, works well for a sitting person, or a standing one, narrowing to the head with the arms at the sides, or folded on the chest. Yet children in arms can't protrude beyond the surface of tusk, and so become flat sketches in the more plausible arms of the swelling curves of the women who enfold them. Only in rare cases has the sculptor used the shape of the object he started with as something we are aware of, both as hovering behind the product, and as something that is completely overcome: the graciously bending Virgin Marys of the Middle Ages, carved from the tusk, are an example of something that uses the curve and the bland glow of the whiteness as part of the end effect.

Small hard things are always what is at the top of their respective pyramids, portable and valuable, what is held to be the flower of the plant, when the plant itself must be sacrificed—and which in turn is sacrificed when the point is to render homage to a person held to be the flowering of other people. In the old days, kings had slaves killed around them, a practice we don't follow any more—and so don't think such practices do them honor. But in the case of the Bactrian Hoard, conveniently, we too like the things sacrificed to the dead: these pieces of gold jewelry would be at the top of our pyramid too. Because we share the world of valuation that held them to be the things most worthy of the most important people, we think them so as well.

Now they have become the small hard things not just of a group of people, but of something much larger: of a whole time. Should the Russian aristocrats of the time of Napoleon stand before us, we wouldn't be able to see their clothing as their clothing, but as "old-fashioned" or "period" clothing—costumes rather than clothing. Their clothing would stand for a whole time. Here, the Bactrian Hoard stands not only for a time, rather than just these individual people, of whom we know nothing, but also for a political entity that didn't exist until thousands of years later, a country on whose soil they were discovered, treasured in the dark of a bank vault as they had been interred in the dark of a tomb, and now sent to the capital of the country that made it possible, at least in theory, to imagine their exposition in a renovated building that has yet to be built, in a city that has yet to be resurrected. They're still small hard things, but what they're small hard things of—the iceberg of which they are the tip—has changed.

Obituaries
News obituaries are one way of creating small hard things, in this case the short, summarizable, narrative of the person's life. It's in obituaries where we see the disconnect between things of interest to the individual and those tiny bits of his or her life that can be integrated into the public museum of the ongoing story of History. So-and-so was a movie star for several years in the 1930s. So-and-so was the secretary of a statesman at an important conference. So-and-so was a mobster convicted of murdering his mistress and the scandal of 1975. So-and-so started the company (unknown) which later became another company (better known). Obituaries are ways of fitting people into a story like a game of dominoes that requires a match to allow it to be fit in: this minor detail of the person's life is how he or she will enter the string of history. So-and-so, we read (unknown), was the third husband of so-and-so (known), only to be supplanted by another and another. How would this person feel about the fact that this would be his claim to fame?

Literary history, or intellectual history, works like obituaries. The givens of intellectual or literary history are as inexorable as the rules of obituaries: a large earthquake qualifies for inclusion, a small one (though it may have cost a number of people their lives) is meaningless. To have gone down with the *Titanic* conveys status; to have gone down in a smaller, unknown ship doesn't merit a mention. Similarly, what was of interest to the individual may have no interest for intellectual or literary history. Most people don't rate a mention, some are footnotes. Even major figures are frozen in positions they wouldn't have recognized. Voltaire is known as the author of *Candide*, not of the works on which he thought his renown would rest, his (to us) unreadable alexandrine neo-classical tragedies. Presumably he'd be aghast at the way literary history, his long-term obituary, treats him.

So literary or intellectual history is a subsequent creation for reasons that the people referred to might well have found incomprehensible, or abhorrent. It's made the way people re-assign the contents of Grandpa's house: it'll only be chance if we think the same things valuable that Grandpa did.

The real Bactrian Hoard

The *Annales* school of history, named for the journal that espoused the movement in the mid-twentieth century, thought it unfair that history would have focused only on "important men." It was the little people, they insisted, in whom history should be told, the more general waves of change, the ebbs and flows of public taste and opinion. At first glance this seems to object to using certain people as stand-ins for others, as their small hard things: the kings, the popes, the prize winners. Literary history, it points out, isn't the list of Nobel Prize winners.

But the objection of this school of history isn't to having small hard things, only to using these particular things as the small hard things. It only objects to using the people whom the people of their time would have agreed were the small hard things of their time: the kings, the leaders. Instead we have to use the people agreeing on the value of the king: they're the ones that created the value, after all. So doesn't that make them more valuable? It's as if, instead of displaying the objects from the Bactrian Hoard, it insisted that the things that these people found important enough to bury in honor of their leaders were chaff, and instead of the jewels, they would display the dust of the bones that once were arrayed with them, the sand and stones from the hill in which they were buried.

Museums in the late twentieth century have shared this focus. They might well have displayed boxes of sand with the label: The Real Bactrian Hoard. This would have been understood as a wry commentary on the fact that museums help convey monetary value on objects. The fact of being shown in a museum makes the value of contemporary artworks shoot up, so that contemplated gifts to museums are frequently shown to the public before they are promised, as being the collection of so-and-so in order to make their value rise—the greater to be the tax write-off when in fact they are given.

The critic Arthur Danto has been the most insistent that this putting on a pedestal actually creates the importance of the thing on the pedestal.[16] It's true that if you can get the people to say that the Emperor's New Clothes are beautiful, it will appear they admire it. But putting a box of sand in a museum is a bit silly: we put things in museums because we take them to be the small hard things, not in order to make them so. If it turns out that museums are trying to create things as small hard things, the betrayal of trust is fully that of the

Emperor and his new clothes. Those artists mesmerized by the power of the market to create something out of nothing are noting the gullibility of the masses, nothing more: those who will agree that the Emperor's clothes are in fact beautiful, even if they see nothing. Those who are less impressed by the fact of museum-ness will look at the box of sand and be indignant: why are we to admire this box of sand and not the sand we passed on the way in? Surely this "artist" doesn't think we're so quiescent we'll agree that anything in a museum is museum-worthy? That anything the Emperor, and his courtiers, say is beautiful material is in fact so, rather than a fraud?

We have to have a reason for putting something in a frame: if we put random things in frames too often, people no longer give credence to the frame. If the museum too often exposes vitrines of fat, or huge constructions of natural materials, or pseudo-stone circles that look as if they've been made by Native Americans but weren't, people will turn away—and largely have done.

We're all looking to find the small hard things in our lives, both physical and abstract, those things we can grab first when we hear the cry of *Fire!*, those things we can transport along the Silk Road. Everything else turns to dust, like the princess whose body was once adorned with gold. Dust is what most of our thoughts and feelings become: each person has his or her own, and so doesn't care about ours. We can't even save our own thoughts, and no one else is interested in them: all of us, all the time, are seeking to find the top of the pyramid of dust, the small hard thing at its summit, which we hold onto for ourselves, and (if we think it sufficiently hard and small) share with others.

Pathetic

The final scene in the classic Orson Welles movie *Citizen* Kane is, literally, pathetic: it induces pathos.[17] In the first scene we see the lips of the dying Charles Foster Kane: "Rosebud," he says, and from his dying fingers falls a snow globe, that shatters on the floor. A nurse comes in and pulls the sheet over his head. At the end of the movie about his life, we see the professional house cleaners. The vast house is full of things with monetary value, bought as if they were "souvenirs," mementos of travel. But they're too many to be souvenirs, small hard things. They don't mean anything. The professionals in charge of numbering them are dismissive because the objects are still in crates, never savored, their acquisition the expression of a compulsion for "the loot of the world" rather than the tips of icebergs. The tips overwhelm the icebergs—or there never were icebergs to begin with. They were acquired for acquisition's sake. (If Kane had been stocking a museum rather than buying for his house, the director of the museum would be thrilled at the number of objects.)

The final scene shows men feeding junk to a great furnace. The object that goes last is a sled, whose brand name is "Rosebud." It's what the dying man said while holding the snow globe; subsequent scenes have shown us the snow of his childhood home, and him playing in the snow with a sled (brand name not divulged). The pathos is that no one but the now-dead man understands the significance of the sled: it was a small hard thing for him, but for no one else. There isn't even any one to look at it, realize that it must have meant something to him: it's consigned to flames by professional rubbish removers. Only the viewer of the film understands—not even the people sent to make a better newsreel, one that captures the "real" Charles Foster Kane, ever understand.

Tag sales (yard sales) escape the pathetic simply because the people putting these things up for sale are still alive, or have indicated they don't want these things any longer: someone else may. These are no longer small hard things. So these now once again neutralized objects are borne home to people's hoards of their own small hard things: they can use this, they've always wanted that. Though they've just acquired them, they fit into a structure of desires and self-realizations.

Estate sales also escape the pathetic: only the things with generally accepted value will be proposed for sale—the jewelry, the china, the rare books. The rest will have been given away or thrown away. Cleaning out Mom and Pop's house may be sad, but it too escapes the pathetic. Probably we know the scale of value to them of the objects in the house: what was valuable, what wasn't. What we don't see with the eye of the estate sale—we know the diamonds are valuable, and the silver—we can see with a version of their eyes.

Kane is pathetic because he has nobody to share his point of view. But in a generation or two, the pathos is lost. We don't mourn the fact that we don't know what the people who, in death, wore the Bactrian Hoard meant to the individuals who dressed them for the grave. At most we seek to understand the generic nature of kingship or chieftanship among the nomads of the time. We're not even seeking the individual. We start from nothing and are happy to get something. We don't find the Gainesborough portraits in the Philadelphia Museum pathetic, bereft as they are of the children who remembered Mom, or the house in which she lived, now all alone on this distant New World shore. Because we're not comparing them with the iceberg that once held them up, they seem merely part of another structure entirely, that of the story of Art History told in every world-class museum, sub-division English 18th century. They're what fill in this blank in the story, like filling up pages in a stamp album: I have one of those, and one of those, and one of those.

Transience
Most of life is as transient as the body of the Tillya Tepe princess. Think of all the words uttered daily, by poets or non-poets that simply wash away, crumble into dust so that we pounce upon the fragments of gold adorning them—and of course many bodies are buried without the gold. When we seek to express the mutability of speech we may, even now in the twenty-first century, grasp at the formulae of the Victorians—what T.S. Eliot called measuring out our lives in coffee spoons, the taking of toast and tea: keeping conversation, as Bernard Shaw had it for Eliza Dolittle, to the subjects of the weather and everyone's health. But most of the mutable speech is less formulaic, at least

nowadays: seeing speech as formulae is itself a way of conceiving of it as small and hard, the form immutable even if the specific isn't.

Listen to people talk.

In the Philadelphia Museum of Art, two egregiously pear-shaped people, a man and a woman (their hips must be twice the size of their chests, both man and woman), lumber through the Thomas Eakins room. "He's sure not good-looking," says the woman of the subject of one of Eakins' merciless warts-and-all portraits: she laughs heartily at her own wit. Her age is indeterminate, perhaps she's 40; her hair is cut like a small girl's, long in the back, bangs in the front. "I'll say," says the man, rolling forward with his beach-like floatation ring, his body, moving forward and slightly back with every step: both wear running shoes. The man, clearly besotted by the woman, chuckles appreciatively. They round the corner, on the way to the monumental Eakins "Gross Clinic" and Augustus Saint-Gaudens' "Angel of Mercy." Here is a vast art deco fireplace. "Now *that* is a fireplace," says the woman, chuckling again at her drollity. The man agrees.

How much of this interchange will survive? How much should?

"Do you have the *New York Times*?" asks someone in a store in upstate New York. "Usually we do, but we're out," says the proprietor.

There's nothing to save in this interchange, any more than this: "Is it going to rain?" "The TV said it would." "I don't see any clouds." "You'd better take an umbrella just in case."

Why should this survive its moment? Thank goodness it doesn't. The standard joke is stale, the standard pleasantry is flat, the standard exchange is functional only. What else should it be? Standard means usual. Language is used in many ways; only certain uses achieve the form, if briefly, of the small and hard—and whether or not they do depends on whether or not people treat them this way. Compared to the situation, a single word may be a small hardness: Henry James was fond of setting up situations where silence welled up behind words, and made them carry the weight of the whole exchange. Or Hemingway. But we can't spend our time reading Henry James or Hemingway. We too have our not-small, not-hard lives to live.

In recent decades academics have been on a rampage to create new sorts of small hard things. The unknown writings of people who led unspectacular lives but left some salvageable traces, daily art forms like embroidery, the utilitarian decorationism of non-Western peoples: all these are rescued from oblivion, put on pedestals, treated like the small hard things we're used to. Scholars grow self-righteous and wild-eyed at the thought that they are giving due credit to under-estimated peoples, genders, and groups. Some grow steely at the thought that the patriarchy has tried to repress these things, hold (say) the household crafts of women as being of lesser importance than male art forms like literature or painting—or that a carved house post of the Yoruba could (can you imagine it?) have once in a less benighted age been held as merely utilitarian, not conforming to the Western idea of art and so of lesser value. Now, we hear, we know better: the most mundane, utilitarian, unappreciated thing can be the same as the high art forms of Western males. Expositions are held, catalogues are written, to rescue from oblivion the small hard things of the worlds of the marginalized.

Which is fine, except that finding more small hard things doesn't change the fact that they wouldn't be small hard things if they in turn didn't represent the tip of their own icebergs, which by definition remain submerged. We can rescue the household crafts of, say, women in North Dakota in the 1880s—but if these are not the tips of their own icebergs, they are too much to consider. A record of all the words that crystallize thoughts to others would be unread, like the *Congressional Record* that preserves every word uttered in Congress, or the books put out yearly in the United States alone: close to half a million, most of them read only by the author and his or her immediate family. Still, the printed form and the cover conveys smallness and hardness, like framing something, the illusion that this stands for more than it is.

Bridges are named after X, highways "dedicated to" Y. The equivalent for roads of a self-published book given to one's family is the road sign on a dirt path in the country saying "Phil Johnson Road." There's the sign. But for this really to be "dedicated to" Phil Johnson, or named after him, we'd probably demand that this be reflected on maps, or in a central town registry—not just be something the family put up on their property. But if nobody cares, what does even official registration with a town confer? Even if it's a real bridge, a public structure, and an official naming ceremony with the governor present, how does this relate to the person of whom it's a small hard thing? He or she likely didn't even live to see it; and what sense does it make for someone to have been turned into a bridge? As much sense as having been turned into a photograph and a pout, like Marilyn Monroe. This isn't eternal fame; it's eternal misrepresentation. But all small hard things are in this sense misrepresentations of their icebergs: if they weren't they wouldn't be small hard things, and you couldn't carry them along the Silk Road.

Mute inglorious Miltons

We think of, say, Emily Dickinson's poems as the small hard things that crystallize and so render external an intense internal life. We can heft the book with all of them: they seem concrete, and more concentrated than the passage of time in the life of the long-ago and now rotted woman: the putting on of clothing and the taking off, the making of jams, the taking of walks. Emily Dickinson has become her poems, the way Marilyn Monroe has become her photograph with the skirt blown up, and the recordings of her face, body and voice on film. The poems aren't an imitation of an inner world, they're a preserving, a pickling. Of course the product isn't the same as the fresh thing: the fresh thing would be long gone.

But the preserves we have form their own realm, the way African masks in a Western museum can't possibly any longer be the small hard things of a particular village, or for that matter this Gainsborough portrait really of a particular person (though the person's name is still attached to it: we'd be equally pleased to have another name entirely). They define a world of preserves, just as the treasure of Tillya Tepe becomes the stuff of the museum world, or less individualized or politicized treasures the stuff of the art market. These things are no longer the small hard things of one woman; they're part of the realm of now-separate small hard things of this sort, just as the grave portraits of Italy and Southern France will some day cease to be, except trivially, the portraits of particular people (we can still say that an Egyptian statue is a portrait of a particular scribe, but no one cares).

Think of a world in which the poems of Emily Dickinson had not been published, or those of Wilfred Owen: for us it would be a different world, a world without Emily Dickinson or Wilfred Owen. They existed, they wrote: we have the small hard things they wrote. Or Sylvia Plath—to name another writer who put his or her life into the form of small hard things, and very nearly was passed by. We have the small hard things we have: who's to say that there aren't other Emily Dickinsons whose works are not published after their death? We needn't think that the only people who led intense inner lives are the ones who translated these into small hard things: how many nomadic chieftans were buried besides the single one we know as the center of the Bactrian Hoard? Even Tutankhamun was a minor, teen-aged pharaoh. Most of the others are lost to us, or plundered long ago. Yet for us, King Tut defines the Egyptians.

The point is not so much that the world might well have (to quote the poet Gray) "mute inglorious Miltons," which it certainly does—but that even the un-mute glorious Miltons are only the tiny percentage of something lost forever. They haven't translated their lives, or transmitted them. The act of preserving has changed the life into a few lines on the page. This is as true of Milton as it is of Joe Smith; we don't compare the poems of Milton with the man, and so it seems to us that we get a lot from Milton and nothing from Joe. In fact we get precious little from Milton either.

Biographies of famous people, say writers, obscure this fact: they point the life towards the work, making it seem inexorable that the vast iceberg of life produced this tip of words. They're written backwards with respect to the way the lives were lived, where great quantities of life were compressed into the lines that had not yet come to be, and so could not be used to justify them. It sometimes seems as if the small hard things redeem the part of the iceberg they stand for: if only I can express how I felt in words, things will be different. But if no one reads this, how is anything different? If someone does read it, how are things different, especially if I no longer feel that way, or am dead? How am I different if my grandson treasures my gold ring? To me it's just my ring; to him it becomes the small hard thing that stands for granddad.

Rolex

Making one set of small hards doesn't guarantee that we won't need to re-organize these later, to make a level beyond that becomes the new small hard. The value of a "college degree" has sunk with the proliferation of them in the United States. Hence the cut-throat competition for a degree from a *well-known* college or university. This isn't so much a market fact—when everybody has a Rolex watch there will have to be a super-Rolex; when every body has a credit card it's time to introduce the Gold, then Platinum cards—as it is a fact of small hard things: in order to be small hard things they can't be so common as to fail to arouse comment.

Indeed, everyone today in wealthy countries has wealth undreamed-of by any but the small hard people of earlier ages: it doesn't satisfy us. We don't say we live better than King Darius of the Persians: we say we don't live as well as X, who is our new small hard standard—probably, in our democracy, a movie star, or athlete, someone whose skills are widely appreciated and so commodifiable as to be saleable in units average people can afford.

So all but very few of our thoughts, feelings, emotions, and reactions, are doomed to crumble away into oblivion. We don't change this fact by saving the small hard things, because the mere existence of small hard things presupposes a vast number of large soft ones that they come to represent and replace. If we could have in front of us the people from *War and Peace*, themselves already harder smaller versions of many real people the way a glass flower is a smaller, harder version of many real flowers, they would be flustered and angry at our interest. We'd want to put their clothes on mannequins in museums, listen to their turns of phrase to see what they are, how Russian aristocrats spoke in the Napoleonic era: to them, they're just communicating, merely getting through the evening; to us every word that drops from their lips is a small hard thing.

They'd be like the girl in the fairy story, the younger of two sisters—the sweet-tempered one. She was sent to the well to fetch water by her domineering mother; an old woman asked her for water; she cheerfully complied. The woman was in fact a fairy, and gave her a gift that was only revealed when the girl reached home and had to answer her shrewish mother's scoldings about why she'd been so late: when she opened her mouth to speak of the woman at the well, there fell from her mouth flowers and jewels. The mother was ecstatic, and sent her older daughter, the ill-tempered one, to the well with a bucket. She too met someone asking for water, this time a young woman rather than the old one she was expecting. And so she replied in her usual form, refusing haughtily. This woman too was the same fairy in another form, and gave the girl a gift as well. When she reached home her mother entreated her to speak: when the girl launched into her story, the nature of the fairy's gift to her was revealed: from her mouth dropped snakes and toads. The story has it that the younger sister was married by a prince, because every time she spoke so many wonderful things fell from her lips. Only the fact is, the story has to end here. Think of the piles of rotting flowers! Where would they find the vases for all of them? And if every word was a jewel or a flower, a few longer stories with their roomfuls of jewels would soon flood the market with diamonds. The museum, full of tips of icebergs, merely reiterates that the icebergs aren't in it. The space outside is to be used for running. Value isn't just in the small hard things: this value is by contrast with something else which the small hard things need—value is in the contrast, both what is saved and what rots away.

If there is value in what we do, it can't be in the what, but in the doing: given that we're fated to be like this, we did what was necessary to be like this. We set goals, and fulfilled them: the point was the process, not the achievement of the goal. In the short run we may need the memories, but at some point we should need only the memory of the memory, trading in all the shelves of "souvenirs" for a more abstract thing, that reminds us we went places, did things. Or perhaps at that point we need nothing more to remind us of this fact.

The running path, on which I am now walking, with a pleasant sense of well-earned tiredness, is part of what makes the value of the Bactrian Hoard: without running, the world that no one but me values, there is no such thing as the collectively valued things within. What I alone do has value, but this isn't because it can one day be exhibited in a museum, or written about in a book: it's because it's part of the world. Value isn't just in small hard things, but of logical necessity in the relationship of these small hard things with the rest of the world from which they are taken, the world in which I run.

6
Running in Barcelona

In Barcelona, I went running my first day—the first one after my arrival, at any rate, and I'd learned never to go running immediately after a few intermittent hours of sleep in an airplane seat. Years ago, not observing this rule, I'd fallen over a curb in the Parisian suburbs where I was staying with a friend and had to limp back to his house to bleed. Worse, I upset his mother when, woozy and disoriented, I almost broke a coffee table by sitting down heavily on it: she talked about it for years afterwards. Because you can stay upright, I learned from that experience, you can't necessarily conclude you should be running. At least not the first day. But after that, runs are recommended. They clear away some of the jetlag cobwebs.

Too, if you move faster than the people around you, and earlier, you get to feel a bit like Superman, swooping around the buildings, even if you stay on the ground. You're up before others too, so it seems you observe them almost from without: you watch them as if from an airplane, small creatures going about their business below. Running in a still-somnolent city gives you a sense of the whole. I like to look at the whole anthill, not be one of the streaming line of ants. It's the position that's most congenial to the position of bemused outsider/participant in which, the decades have taught me, I feel most at home.

That first morning, it wasn't quite day when I left for my run. I ran through the artificial light of the shopping streets leading back to the Plaça de Cataluña. I passed a few people walking by the shops closed with metal pull-downs and one on a bicycle, then ran across the smaller cobbles where bleary-eyed visitors drew rolling suitcases click click click on their way to the airport bus or to their hotel, as I had done the day before.

On the Rambla, the wide promenade street that sloped gently down to the Mediterranean, the light of the graying dawn wasn't strong enough to turn off the automatic streetlights. I had expected it to be deserted at this hour: that's part of the illusion of power of running at early hours through empty streets. Instead, the smooth, wide marble pavement down the center of the street was full of groups of clearly inebriated young men, and a few women, singing loudly, hanging on each other. For me it was Sunday morning; for them it was the bitter end of Saturday night. Some hooted as I ran by or swerved around them. I waved, smiled, or ignored them, depending on their tone and whether or not I felt like interacting. Who was invading whose space?

As I descended the slope towards the sea, the late-Saturday-nighters became fewer: there were just a handful of people hurrying to the metro, and I had once again room to run without weaving in and out. I picked up my feet around and past the Christopher Columbus pillar, taking care not to trip on the curbstones— it had, after all, been a curbstone that had been my undoing those many years ago outside of Paris. So far, I thought, so good, though since the last few minutes down the Rambla had been downhill, I reminded myself I shouldn't be getting too cocky. My body was only half-accustomed to the time change; probably I was running on adrenaline and shock.

In only a few seconds here at the base of the Rambla, slowing to decide which direction to go in, I could sense the difference in the light, the sun trying to pull itself slowly out of the sea. In one direction was what looked like an old-fashioned port building, next to me the re-furbished 19th century customs building, all spandrels and statues. I ran by an old-time boat, part of a museum the sign said, past more modern sculptures on a sort of raised promenade area, by the side of the water. And then I broke free of the smaller shapes and saw, across the main road, the palms silhouetted against the buildings being born again into the strengthening light, their facades crystallizing in the rising sun opposite them. It seemed that day was coming to be around me, as if I were conjuring the light through my motions.

At the end of the sidewalk I curved back into town, taking as my goal the road that led to the main park that I'd located to the east of the Barrio Gotico. Somehow I missed the road; later I realized I should have turned right sooner than I did. Still, I had a general idea of where I was going. In running, goals are approximate, as the point is the run itself. Only I hadn't realized just how approximate this goal was: after a few quick turns I found myself abruptly, and somewhat puzzlingly, in an area I hadn't seen on any map. It could have been a less commercial version of Paris's Latin Quarter of perhaps the 1920s: drabber, with fewer cafes and shops and more apartments, though all still shuttered over in the early Sunday morning, their facades with blank sectioned curtains of metal where their life would later show, like eyelids opening to reveal the animal within.

In only a few steps, it seemed—in reality, a small number of blocks that went by quickly— I was in a small square. Though, I marveled, it wasn't square: it was lozenge-shaped, as if the street had taken a deep breath that pushed back the buildings: the plaza in the middle began and ended gradually at the ends, and was only a slight expansion in the street, perhaps trebling its width rather than having inserted into it a full-fledged sharp-edged shape of a proper piazza. Still, it was big enough for wrought iron lampposts, and for benches, now deserted in the stage-set before me. The façades, which continued to look French to me, were residential, but all silent, each window still blinded by its shutter, the people within asleep. The gray of the sky by now was white, but the sun had yet to solidify: everything was perfectly visible, but as if only just having crystallized from the darkness. This time and place belonged, it seemed, to me.

I was so charmed by the way this street had so unexpectedly taken a breath and gently expanded, here on this square with its florid black-painted wrought-iron lamps, its benches in which no one sat, this gentle opening between the buildings in which I found myself alone, that I slowed to a walk, the better to savor the last diaphanous layers of the night now all but gone, the silence, the unexpected blessing of this tiny world that I was merely in transit through and that, to others when the sun was up and children played and old people sat on the benches, was home. I felt the heat of my chest rising up to my face, the altered sense of my leg muscles walking rather than running, felt the puffs of my own breath, the uneven stones under my feet.

And then suddenly I was aware of something that shouldn't be there. Perhaps it was a faint motion of the air, an all but silent sound, the sixth sense of the presence of another person—and I stepped quickly to one side and whirled into the embrace of a tall young man pressed behind me, his head protected by a black motorcycle helmet, his feet silenced by white tennis shoes, his arms ready to go around my neck.

I had thrown him off balance by my split-second-too-soon turn, and his hands flailed at the air. It was as if he'd coalesced from the strengthening light, like the façades of the buildings, the iron filigree of the lamps—or, like the square itself, had simply breathed himself into existence. What side street had he been hiding in? Where had he come from? I had seen the whole square and there was no place he could have hidden. Then there he was, pressed against me, ready to strike.

Strangely enough, my first impulse wasn't to run or pull away. As if coming up from the depths between the arms of someone treading water, I didn't move backwards. Instead, in an instant, I tensed, balled my fists, and began yelling at the top of my lungs, still in this abrupt intimacy almost like an embrace. Thankfully, it wasn't as in dreams, where we find ourselves unable to make a noise and wake moaning, worrying the other person in the bed with us who caresses us and soothes us. I was really yelling.

Perhaps what I was saying wasn't the most macho thing I could have chosen, but of course it all went far too quickly for choice: this was pure impulse. Probably I should have yelled "You bastard, I'll kill you!" Instead, I screamed, over and over, "I have no money, let me go, I have no money." I knew he might not understand but I wasn't about to yell it in Spanish: part of the shock would be a language he wasn't expecting. I didn't see a weapon, saw that he was almost as tall as I: In the split-seconds of yelling I was able to wonder he would be so daft as to try and mug a runner, and a big one at that—was he on drugs, not thinking? I wasn't at all a logical target. My feeling was as much one of disbelief as of threat: what was happening wasn't just abrupt, but senseless, completely irrational. The yelling and the split-second-too-soon whirl had done their work, perhaps also the English. Abruptly I was aware that he had taken a step back, his hands held up in an "okay I give up" gesture. His change of stance didn't register immediately; I continued to yell and stand my ground, as if wanting to continue a conversation, make my point, convince him of something: rationality should, after all, triumph. Then the import of his gesture hit me and I turned and ran, though unhurriedly, cursing as I did so as if merely continuing on my way.

What was I feeling? I wasn't sure. Probably I was feeling rueful, that I could have been so stupid—for many years I'd been hearing stories about "watch your purse in the Barrio Gotico"—yet still, I thought, I hadn't been foolhardy. I'd asked in the hotel if it was safe to go running, and the man had been reassuring, treating my question as verging on ridiculous. Of course, he'd said: You're moving. I'd neglected to ask what happened if I momentarily stopped running.

I knew that the longer I ran, the less this incident would matter, shrinking in size relative to the rest of the run, becoming only one event among many others. If I simply continued my earlier project of finding the park, this momentary violence averted, this conjuring out of nowhere of someone who wished me harm, would merely be a hiccup, a blip. My body was surprisingly cooperative, neither jerky with the nervous energy of a rush nor dumping me in an energy bottom-out as it might as a reaction to a stress situation, apparently ready for a nice leisurely run.

So I ran and ran along nondescript but no longer so narrow streets, going by instinct if somewhat blindly, telling myself the park had to be here somewhere if I just kept going—and keeping going was the point, after all. Façades, more façades, quiet streets, wider than the one that had threatened to be my downfall. Their very monotony soothed me. And then abruptly I was in a long piazza down the middle of an avenue that had opened up at right angle to the street I'd been running on, a great stone expanse like a sweeping away of the buildings, dotted with absurdly arabesqued lampposts and marked at one end by a huge brick arc of triumph. Looking down, I saw it inclined gently down to what was clearly the very park I had been looking for, where I entered the gates and felt the gravel crunch under my feet.

By now it was full daylight with other people crossing from one side of the park to another, with even another runner or two, middle-aged men on their Sunday once-a-week exercise routine. I could feel the near attack subsiding to the place of a bubble in a piece of blown glass, still there, but imprisoned within the now sufficiently longer run. Yet if I let myself go into this bubble, this now-contained world, the questions swarmed: How bad could it have been? Could I have been knocked to the sidewalk with bruises, a broken bone, or a concussion, my vacation ruined on its first day? Could I have been killed? And then the world around me caught this bubble and froze it once again within the solid substance of the world and the motions of my body through them, containing it in the domesticated palm trees, the nineteenth-century Medievalesque building now a museum, the Victorian greenhouses filled with palms, the paint chipping off onto the panes of glass, and the cascade fountains where white dolphins spouted water from their mouths in the early morning light.

Later I realized I should have studied the map in my room that morning a bit more: exiting the park, I should have gone straight, by the Estacion de

Francia. By this point I was ready to have the run over, and in five minutes I would have been back at the ornate Correos building, my turn to go back to the cathedral and my hotel. Yet never having seen this street from the other direction, I didn't realize it was the right one, and so, on exiting another set of gates that were on the side 90 degrees to the one I'd entered, I turned left, curving, curving, following railroad tracks—running, running, by now it seemed forever. Still, after another quarter of an hour through blank, uninteresting streets, I came up on the opposite side of the square with the Correos, and I slowed and walked.

I had achieved my goal: the sheer length of my run, the endless anonymous streets had swallowed that moment in the square when suddenly I was aware that someone was behind me and had whirled. What if I hadn't turned? No one would have come to my help: the windows, though hovering above me, were covered, the people inside asleep: real life had not yet started, I had been trying to claim for my own this border area with the night, something they instinctively avoided.

Directional
What overwhelmed me later in the day, when I allowed my mind to go back to this moment, was a consciousness of the directional nature of things. I saw again the motorcycle helmet of my mugger, protecting him against what he was about to inflict on me; felt the eerie split-second of the sense of nearness of another man, tight behind me and ready to do me harm. In the center of the helmet I had seen the small window of his face, shrouded in the almost-darkness of the square itself and of the shadow cast by the brim. Suddenly, there he'd been there behind me, taking advantage of the fact that we none of us have eyes in the back of our heads. Nor did he, the back of his own head cradled in the protection of his helmet.

There was a whole blind world behind the back of my head. The threat had come to be within this shadow world; only by turning did I make it suddenly enter the light. There had been none of the gradual smallness-to-largeness of the way people usually, gradually, enter our field of vision, the softness-to-loudness that announces imminent contact, allowing us to turn so gradually that we are rarely conscious of our repositioning to meet the thing we meet. Even the exceptions to this more usual coming-into-consciousness seem to prove the rule: Oh! we exclaim as we look up to see someone standing before us. You startled me! And the other person apologizes; we laugh a heh-heh, perhaps put our hands on our chests, and then go back to what we were doing, feeling the thumps of our heart subside.

People aren't supposed to surprise us; they have to give us fair warning of their approach. We teach people these rules, and they know they must abide by them: make some noise as you approach, cough a bit when you're near the room, begin to speak a few seconds earlier than you need to in order to give the other person time to re-orient, to come to terms with your presence, to re-assume the face-to position of interaction. If the offender to the rules is a child, as it frequently is, we explain that this was wrong, they need to knock, or somehow make their presence known. Don't startle me, child! we say. Or: you're too quiet! We deal with the envelope of blindness that surrounds us by stringently enforcing the elaborate rules for avoiding it, and allowing people to forget it's there. In the world of light and civilized interaction, we can minimize this blindness, even be unaware of it.

This encounter in the otherwise deserted square brought out the fact of the weakness we try so hard to hide by the simple expedient of leading with our area of strength. It's as if we were all snakes that capture our prey by bringing our fangs around to a frontal business position, are feared for our venom and our deadliness, and yet can be rendered impotent by a pair of human fingers squeezing us behind the head, a boot on our spine. This mugger was the boot on my spine, going for a position of which polite society, normal interactions with people, do their best to deny the existence, minimizing them and rendering them non-existent, giving us respect, the time to re-orient—so that through years of getting used to people avoiding the darkness around us, we come to forget it's there.

The world, I suddenly understood, wasn't filled with light; it was mostly dark, the night merely reclaiming its own, which was the largest constituent of the day—the interleaving of blindness, weakness, and darkness that we constantly keep behind us, like a nineteenth-century woman re-arranging the train of her dress and flipping it in a practiced way behind her, so well and so frequently she's not even aware of doing it, the snake re-arranging its body with a flick. Yet our eyes are trained to seek this light, and so they simply put behind them the great cushions of night we trail, and usually forget. We are creatures that have to slither around so we face one another from the front, we establish elaborate rules to hide the slithering, to make sure it can happen in an unproblematic fashion. The clock only starts when we're in position, so we simply remove from consideration a lot of life: we take care to let the other snakes slither around so that they face us head-on.

In war, of course, we not only don't forget this darkness, we use it as the basis of what we do. It's a given that we want to come up behind people. So do muggers. The rules of our normal world hide this other world, the world of those who identify weakness in order to exploit it. What we therefore tend to ignore, under normal circumstances, is precisely the world in which this must be prevented: find the weakness and exploit it.

In wrestling, if your opponent winces when you put pressure on his shoulder, you do it again, rather than excusing yourself and avoiding the spot. Yet with social weaknesses, avoiding and excusing is precisely what we do. Good manners consists of avoiding them when they can be predicted, and immediately relaxing our hold when we hit one unawares. We avoid talking about someone's divorce, the death of a loved one (unless it seems they want to talk about either); we ask questions in ways that allow them to tell their stories the way they want. Not: Haven't you gotten married *yet*? But: Tell me what's new. This latitude allows other people the time and space to maneuver around to face us, putting behind them once again the world of the blind spot, the back of the head—the logical obverse of the world of vision and clarity, the world where we are turned toward someone, rather than away, where we face them with our front, not the back. Every front implies a back; all vision implies blindness; all order implies chaos.

Awareness
The sense of awareness of the blind world behind continued through the rest of my time in Barcelona. The next day, determined to avoid the dark underground transportation system given the strengthening spring up on the surface, I steered a pedestrian course due West, cutting across the Rambla that I had seen in the near-dawn, spotted with weaving students hanging on each others' shoulders. Now, in the light of full-fledged day, it was full of stalls that faced the direction of the people drifting down the center. To someone such as me cutting across them—or, as I did briefly, walking down their backs and then wandering a bit (the museum didn't open for a while yet: museums only open in the prime of day)—they too seemed relentlessly directional, the people agreeing to stay in front where they were supposed to so as not to see the ugly backs with protruding parts.

Here on the Rambla, the flower shops of the top of the slope gave way to pet shops—turtles, fish, and lizards—and then to sidewalk artists. These too were directional, both temporally and spatially, with their backs or off time hidden from view, either actually or as the result of the fiction produced by what we call politeness: people just knew to look away. They were painted mimes who sat (I later realized) all day, and then came back the next day, and the next, to collect the Euros put in their pots by the strollers. One was a man who made up like a cowboy with his face the same sort of metallic gold as his clothes and hat. I saw him without the hat, his face paint ending at the hat line, smoking a furtive cigarette on his break, before re-assuming his motionless position; two women were angels who re-arranged their hands and their wings but put on their costumes in the side street; there was a Death with a scythe. There was one I never saw in an "off" moment. It seemed to be a man without a head, a hat and glasses suspended in the space where a head was. Yet the theatrically "well-dressed" body underneath (spats, a black bow tie) periodically moved and re-arranged itself, its white-gloved hands re-folding or gesturing. Perhaps it was really a small woman whose head ended at what seemed to be the base of the neck. Surely no one could crick his or her neck so successfully at a 90 degree angle, and hide the bulge under the shoulder of a shirt.

That morning, I continued across the Rambla down an otherwise featureless street where Japanese tourists were lining up to see what little there was to see of the Art Nouveau (Modernista, as it's called in Castillian) Palacio Guëll, which quickly became endless t-shirt shops, and then commercial before, in ten or fifteen minutes, continuing up the hill. I knew this had to lead to the museum hill I'd seen on the map. As the crow flew, it wasn't far. Only I wasn't in the air, and didn't fly.

Soon the street produced a funicular up the hill, which I had vowed to avoid, and the proper street curved off and back down. There was, however, a thin footpath of concrete, winding back and forth through the weeds up the hill: clearly this wasn't the front entrance, and because it involved trudging up a steep hill, wasn't even the way people were supposed to get up to the top. But of course, that's why I liked it: show me the way you're supposed to do something and I'll find the other way.

Slinging my jacket over my shoulder—by now it was hot—I continued up. The path led up to behind a sort of sports center, or rather its fence, all of which was deserted; I passed a woman with a dog whom she coaxed to go pee-pee in the bushes, overgrown with weeds. Still, with sturdy shoes, my physical well-being, and certainty of my general direction—which was, after all, up—I continued. At the graffiti-covered sports center—abandoned or just in the moment not in use?—the path itself petered out and became dirt. Still, there were signs of other people before me who, having come to this place, merely continued on, making another path. I did this too, conscious all the time that this isn't the way one was supposed to get on top of this hill. Then suddenly I was on a proper road, with a proper bus stop, before a proper building, with trees and sidewalks and once again the feeling that the world had been allowed to re-arrange itself to meet me face to face.

Even this wasn't the front entrance to this hill, but merely a stop on a bus route: nearby was the Miró Museum, which I passed under the trees. There were no other walkers. And when finally I had curved around endless shaded loops, following a sign, I came upon a small park where a dozen people where doing Tai Chi. I asked a man, was this building the Catalan Museum of Art? No, he said. That's—and he thought—the Cartographic museum. Maps, he added. And he pointed me in the right direction. Once again I was coming, it seemed, from the side: up one staircase, then another, roads leading in several directions—and it wasn't until some minutes later, sweating, that I stood at the top of the steps and surveyed the vast expanse that were meant to be traversed in the opposite direction, beholding the axis of front, the fangs of this snake that I had crept up on from the back.

Here was the cascade of steps falling down to the vast exposition expanse, dotted with temporary buildings, the huge Venetian belltower, the rest of the Plaça de España that stretched beyond, and the whole huge city stretching up into the hills, as if the steps were the water from a faucet filling a great bathtub of the city's buildings. From the side, I had found the front, where others came to begin with.

Later, the jet lag massing for another attack, sitting between the sun-struck palm trees in the hugely overstuffed leather chairs in the hallway of the museum, I was once again strongly aware of the world I trailed, the world of darkness, blindness, and weakness, and of the way things around me conspired to keep from me the secret existence of this world. All the chairs here pointed inwards so that people naturally faced each other, and the open space, rather than the walls or a blind alley, produced the sense of a Someplace that we were all part of. Even the orientation of the building, and its construction, played to this sense of everything being frontal, frontality meeting frontality. The entrance had been at the top of the hill at the top of the sea of steps, not hidden behind the back; the ticket window was through the main door, clearly visible; the openings to the medieval galleries were off the main hallway, rather than off a hidden back corridor. The whole building was constructed so as to make sight, light, rationality, and frontedness seem ineluctable.

And, pulling myself up from the chair and entering the galleries with my wave of weariness past, I remained aware of the maneuverings, the sheer work, necessary to keeping this fiction alive, of all the things we do and take for granted to remain in the light, to hide our blindness. Instead of turning naturally toward another person, I now saw myself switching around to my back the area of my blindness. I turned my blindness away from the young woman sitting on the stool at the entrance, who hid her own area of blindness against a wall, smiled in a friendly way as I entered her sphere so as to reassure her the interaction would be unproblematic, presented her my ticket at arm level to meet her sight, which she turned to me, then turned to the paintings, whose backs were against the walls, offering themselves for my inspection.

All motion seemed determined by maneuvering around the blindness. Before backing up from a picture I looked behind me to make sure I wasn't going to hit someone, and navigated around the gallery, trailing the blind pocket, into which the mugger had suddenly materialized, like a large bag of air. It seemed to me like the backpacks extending out from the unthinking students I saw on the metro in the next few days who turned their bodies as if unaware that their reach backwards had now been multiplied, and that every twist of their shoulders translated into a swinging arc of heaviness they themselves were unconscious of. The backpacks were a new addition to their blindness, so they were clumsy; the blindness itself, however, is something we maneuver adroitly.

In the *Tractatus*, Wittgenstein shows a picture of an eye with a sort of balloon coming out from it, as if the eye were a pair of lips that had blown it up, and remarks: the visual field is not like this.[18] It's in the context of his saying that the world we see is everything, that if we wrote a book called "The World as I Found It" it would include feet, legs, waist, chest, and hands, but not the eye itself. If this is not the visual field, it is however an excellent drawing of the bubble behind us, a drawing of our blindness, the area into which the mugger had abruptly appeared. Or at least his appearance had made clear to me its existence, otherwise so easy to lose from consciousness, like the blind spot on the highway into which, occasionally and to our detriment, automobiles suddenly pop into view.

Plaça Real

What we're "supposed" to do: that's frequently the code word in the world for staying on the front side of things, meeting the other snakes head-on. It's not only spatial, with the world arranged in patterns where we have to stay on the principal axis, come up on things from the correct side, enter the front door, go up the main steps, and sense the path we're to follow. Like the ideal time for jogging, it's also temporal. Two days later I sat just after sunrise in the Plaça Real off the Rambla, its arcades empty and not yet awakened. The restaurants had yet to put out their café tables and chairs, and the shop owners stood before half-opened metal shutters with a hose in their hands, making puddles of water on the stones that ran into the gutters. I sat in the strengthening sun and watched it all come to life, watched the sun touch the top of the so-manicured palm trees in the middle, the delivery vans of fresh fish and seafood come zipping close to my chair, that was bolted to the stones, in order to pull up in front of the restaurants, idle for a few minutes, and then pull away; the fountain, splashing over the cast-iron maidens supporting its bowls, all the round of the day's chores beginning, slowly, to turn. I could of course be here, but clearly I wasn't meant to be: the preparations for the ball aren't the point, only the effect of the princess as she sweeps down the staircase. Watching her put on her jewelry and her face is illicit.

I have known since childhood that it's precisely these backsides of things that I want to see, these times when I'm not "supposed" to be someplace. This is the point of view of the artist, the thinker, the intellectual, part of life but at the same time removed from it, ready with reflection or analysis but unwilling to be part of the sweating round of the lives led by people for whom the front is the only possible entrance, the full-lit day the only time.

My time of day is not the full-lit day of people going about their daily round. It's before all that, just at sunrise, where each moment changes the light and renders all strange. My place is not in the center of things, ascending the main staircase, but rather on the edges, walking through the deserted arcades that later will be enlivened with tourists, or sitting to watch the delivery vans zip in with the food that, later, unreflecting diners will consume, thinking it simply happened to come here. I'm the one who runs where others will later walk on the endless cycle of their daily chores, and then slows down for silent squares just after dawn.

Yet the mugger reminded me that this is merely the Little League of outsidership: those like muggers are the Major League. I am merely playing at tasting the blindness: they live within it. My encounter with the person wishing me harm who had purposely used my blindness against me reminded me that my intellectual's pride was hollow. Compared to him, I was the rankest amateur. I can't compete with the real experts, those who not only taste but live within the bubble of our weakness, blindness, and darkness, renounce the illusion of clarity and meaning to flourish within the irrational world. Though I taste the world of light and clarity at its edges, I'm as tied to this world as those who, as a matter of self-evident course, wait until noon to eat at the tables that will come to fill up my world with noise and purpose, the once-deserted arcades of what will later be the full-lit expanse, off limits to delivery vans and filled with the sun-struck trees, the tourists, and the splashing fountain, of the Plaça Real.

6
Running in the Eastern Sierras

The sun hasn't risen yet in the Deep Springs Valley of California in the eastern Sierras. My jogging shoes, still placed deliberately as I try to walk silently past the circle of one-story buildings that constitutes Deep Springs College, raise only slight puffs in the pre-dawn dust. It's dry here in the high desert; I pass a landscaped triangle at the base of the small dirt loop that the service vehicles drive on, set with cacti and shards of rock from the mountains up on the Westgard Pass. A few steps more and I am at the cattle guard, stepping carefully along its bars so I don't twist my ankle. My wife calls it a "Teddy-guard," as my younger son, as well as the cattle, is afraid of it. One of the two dogs that usually spends the night on the porch behind the dormitory to my right, home to all 25 of the all-male students of Deep Springs College, stretches, trots over with a jingle of license plates, and nuzzles my hand. Now I am on the dirt road leading to the end of the ranch connecting to California Highway 148, the only asphalted road through this remote valley that, save for Deep Springs Ranch and College, is uninhabited—at least by people. We have livestock on the ranch, with coyotes in the valley, countless snakes, and, according to report, at least a transient golden eagle, seen one day soaring high above the valley floor.

Probably I won't see any cars at all on it at all during my early-morning run. For that matter, cars are rare here at any hour. Sometimes at night I stand out on the dirt road behind my house, a house for visiting faculty members such as I am, sandwiched between dining hall ("the BH," Boarding House) and one-story Main Building (classrooms, mail room, store rooms, administration: everything), and watch the amazingly low canopy of dark sky and countless stars. I know a car is coming because the headlights begin to blink at the top of the ridge as the car carrying them negotiates the switchbacks. I can always see when it begins the descent into the valley, as they become more constant and then drift along the thread of road that will take them up the other side.

That end of this small (about 15 miles by 5) valley where the sun is trying to come up leads to the Oasis Valley and to Nevada, over the Gilbert Pass. The Pass is curving and with some vertiginous drop-offs (don't look down) but nowhere near as narrow as the Westgard Pass at the other end of the valley. The Westgard Pass leads to more of California: the Owens Valley, now not quite as arid as it used to be. In 2006, Los Angeles was forced by court order to allow a some water to run back through the Owens River, where it creates a large green snake with furry sides of trees and grasses twisting through the sagebrush. Still, the water is only loaned back, not given: it's re-diverted back to Los Angeles down at Lone Pine, through the Los Angeles aqueduct that dessicated the valley in the early years of the 20th century to feed the future of the thirsty city on the other side of the Mojave desert. The lake at the southern end of the Owens Valley, denied its feeder rivers for almost a century, now appears on maps as "Owens Dry Lake" and causes dust storms when the wind picks up. Most people outside of California know about the big Los Angeles water grab from the movie *Chinatown*, though there it's only a backdrop to Jack Nicholson's stylish hats, Faye Dunaway's shellacked and now so-dated elegance, and the final line: "Forget it, Jake. It's Chinatown."

Still, Los Angeles, more than 200 miles away, hovers over our world. The city owns much of the Owens Valley. Right over the Westgard Pass from Deep Springs, descending into the Owens Valley, the signs say: "No Trespassing, Property of the City of Los Angeles." Even a smallish vacant lot between two houses in the sleepy town of Lone Pine, where we stayed at the Dow Vista Motel (host, in bygone days, to luminaries like John Wayne, shooting movies and toward the end commercials in the odd rocks known as the Alabama Hills across the road), also says: Property of the City of Los Angeles. You look up and it's still only a neighborhood of small one-story houses in the dryness.

The Westgard Pass from Deep Springs Valley over to the Owens Valley is so narrow at one point that only one car can pass at a time: the rocks have been blasted away, but not enough for two lanes of traffic. It's on the straightaway on the eastern edge of the Westgard Pass too where the world's oldest living things grow: bristlecone pines, ugly twisted trees, mostly trunks with a few green tufts, clinging to the sides of the White Mountains. We visited them in a raging snowstorm; it was May after all, and unpredictable. The oldest of them is about 4,000 years old.

Irrigation

The dirt road here in front of me is soaking wet, at least in huge patches: the irrigation lines are at work in the ranch fields on both sides, chit-chitting away and spewing gray plumes of spray across what soon, with the sun up, I know will be the intense green of the alfalfa fields. I see them at their greenest on lazy afternoons when, with my two sons off playing somewhere, I go down to the tire swing (the one you lie in, hung horizontally via nylon cords up to the tree branch) and swing lazily in the shade of the line of trees by one of the fields. Behind me is the dairy barn; in front the fields, and the cockeyed regularity of the shooting-in-various-directions but identically high plumes of white water, struck into incandescence by the afternoon sun that begins just beyond the overhanging branches of the trees. Beyond the green fields cavort horses. Beyond them, the gray desert. And then first one ridge of mountains, then the higher snowy line of the Sierras.

Sometimes on my morning run I see a couple of my students, shrouded in sweatshirts with hoods, out early bent over the irrigation lines on these fields. Come harvest time the farmer, himself a former Deep Springs College student with tattoos, big "guns" (biceps), and a farmer's tan—the polar opposite, in physical terms, of the weedy students—will be out there with the bailer that leaves the square-edged droppings of hay bales in his wake, its lights blazing in the dark. Today, however, I seem to be the only one up. Except for the dog. In the seven weeks I spent as a faculty member at Deep Springs College I never learned to differentiate between the two very similar sort-of-collie farm dogs that can be found anywhere at any time, chasing the cattle, sleeping by the dormitory, or begging at the picnic tables outside the BH, where, as the weather warms up, the students and faculty members typically bring their plates to eat. Now this one is off in the fields, following me in a ragged parallel that changes shape depending on what he finds in the grass and what catches his interest.

It's cold; I pull my hands into my sweatshirt. It's the end of May but still there's frost in the mornings around some of the irrigation pipes. The puddles on the dirt road left by the irrigation plumes are unevenly spaced; it seems accident which plumes reach the road, and from which side, and which don't. Perhaps they just need alignment, some attention from the two students whose labor commitment is to the irrigation lines.

The students rotate jobs, which in addition to irrigation lines and farmhands, include milking and slaughtering cows (the "dairy boys"), working in the kitchen to prepare food and wash dishes, feeding the cows, and other normal ranch chores. Two of them are range-riding cowboys, and they have a longer commitment than students with other jobs: when the older one leaves the college after two years, he has to agree to come back the following summer, on pay, to be the "senior cowboy" when they take the herd up in the mountains. Cowboy jobs, I hear, are different than the other labor commitments: aspirants have to write an essay explaining why they want to be cowboys.

It's the cowboy aspect of Deep Springs that seems to catch the public's imagination, even though only 10% of the student body works as cowboys, and there are many other chores on a ranch than riding herd on the largest form of livestock. Cowboys and a setting sun are pictured on the publicity post card that sits in stacks in the main building, next to the publicity pamphlet (the cover, a lovely picture of the valley, says "'The most selective and innovative college in the world'—*New York Times*"). An article in *Le Monde2* a couple of years ago was entitled "Heidegger chez les Cow-Boys." Perhaps it's the alliteration of talking about a "cowboy college" that makes this a popular way of referring to Deep Springs—at least, by people who do refer to it.

Nobody we talked to outside of academic circles seemed to know much about the place. My wife, for example, not an academic, first heard of Deep Springs first through a not-completely-complimentary article in the *New Yorker* a couple of years ago;. The college gains its label of "most selective" for the ca. 200 applications for fewer than 15 slots in each class, though it doesn't do much by way of recruiting. One student told me other colleges sent glossy booklets, DVDs, follow-up phone calls: Deep Springs sent a single postcard with "Wish you were here" scrawled across the back. The postcard has a cowboy on the front.

Perhaps the French are the most up to speed on the subject of this strange little place. The *Le Monde* article, to be sure, started less than authoritatively by saying the college was in Nevada, which it isn't—it's miles over the California border, in Inyo County, California. Inyo County, which advertises itself as "the other side of California," is to be sure a California most people, including Californians, are completely unaware of, the dessicated Eastern slopes of the Sierras and a few smallish valleys to the east of that. Without the LA water grab, locals told me that the Owens Valley would undoubtedly be much more developed than it is, and the near-total isolation of Deep Springs College, just over the pass, at an end.

While we were at Deep Springs, a crew of two journalists/cameramen arrived from the French television station "Canal +" in Paris, to film a *reportage* on the college. Talking with them, I could understand why the French would think this was Nevada: these young men had flown from Paris to Washington, D.C., then changed planes immediately for Las Vegas, then driven the four hours up and around Death Valley in order to film the cows being milked that evening. They slept in the guest rooms in the main building, filmed a class the next morning, and then repeated the trip in the opposite direction. Perhaps the reporters from *Le Monde* failed to see the bullet-pocked metal sign as the irrigated fields of the Oasis Valley took over from the free range cattle grazing lands of Nevada, saying "Welcome to California."

Cowboy lunch

Certainly the cowboys are the most picturesque of the labor positions, wearing functionally what elsewhere is a costume, or an affectation: hat, spurs ("they don't hurt the horse," one of the assured me), boots and sometimes chaps. We came back early from Death Valley the first weekend to go see the roping and branding down by the lake, at the other end of the valley, where the corrals are located. We arrived just before lunch; they still had about a hundred calves to go. It was the day before Mother's Day; one of the students joked that the distraught mother cows, lowing in anguish at being bereft of their calves, were getting a hell of a Mother's Day present.

The student cowboys by this point in the semester were pretty good with the lassos, but the other students helping were doing this for the first time and had to be exhorted to hurry up, or do this/do that by the middle-aged man who actually ran the farm. His adult son, a better cowboy than any of the students, helped with the lassoing: the goal was the calf's back leg, the better to pull their legs out from under them and get them lying on the ground. Then two students run at the calf and hold it down (sometimes it stands up; you grab it around the stomach and thump it back on the dirt) while other students run for the branding iron with the upside-down T.

The castrating of the males, also part of this process, was the responsibility of the foreman's 17-year-old daughter. One of the students told me he thought this was a conscious decision on the foreman's part: "you never look at her the same way again after you've seen her rip the balls out of a steer," he noted. The procedure seems to be this: you cut off the end of the scrotum (two students are still holding the calf down), pop out the balls, and then reach down to get as much of the tubing as possible. Then you yank; the testicles and tubes come right out. I've heard of people eating these, but the balls at Deep Springs are merely thrown in the dirt. When I asked this ball-busting teenager later about her technique, she said: "Yanking rather than cutting makes it heal faster." Then the empty sack of the bellowing animal got a spray of something antibiotic and antiseptic, and the calf ran lowing away into the calf pen.

Other students that day had their normal chores back at the ranch. Some arrived at lunch time with food: cowboy lunch, I thought, thinking of the songs we'd been listening to over, and over, and over, on the way to, through, and back from Death Valley. My wife, Meg, had bought a CD of a singer named Michael Martin Murphy, whose hit "Wildfire" she'd loved back in Junior High, in Buck's County, Pennsylvania. Now, we read, he was coming to the town of Bridgeport in the next county up, Mono County, to sing, billed as "the man who sang 'Wildfire'." Meg could identify with that.

We couldn't go to the concert (too late in the summer) but we listened to Michael Martin Murphy sing cowboy songs day in and day out for almost two months: children love repetition. The first song on the CD (I soon came to dread it) was actually called "Cowboy Logic": "he's got a simple solution to just about anything: if it's a horse, ride it; if it's a job, do it; if it's a dollar, spend it—afore it burns a hole down in them jeans." But Murphy was laying on his cowboy twang so thick that it turned out Teddy, 4, understandably thought the song was about not Cowboy Logic but Cowboy Lunch. We liked the idea, and made it Cowboy Lunch instead. And down at the corral we were finally getting real cowboy lunch.

Despite my annoyance at listening to these songs over and over, I found their plaintive sounds (and the lyrics I'd finally "get" about the tenth time around) strangely moving. They become wedded to the landscapes through which we listened to them. For me, they're the sounds that accompany the sun setting over the rim of Death Valley, the slow ascent from the Owens Valley up to the first switchbacks of the Westgard Pass, the Tioga Pass into Yosemite, the Sonora Pass from Tahoe. They make clear that cowboys are the bottom of the totem pole. The songs are all about lonely, unwanted men who die solitary deaths, and—contrary to their wishes—are buried alone on the lone prair-ee, or never see their beloved mother again, or are ambushed by Indians, or are out of money, out of work, and out of luck. "What am I doin' here?" asks one song, and it seems emblematic of them all.

Being a cowboy is a loser's proposition, even these songs admit. You're a traveling hand, eternally looking for work, your butt sore from the saddle, liable to fall from your horse into a stampede, underpaid by bosses who only want long hours for cheap wages, unable to save a dime, and with the closest attachment a mother you haven't seen for years or a sweetheart far far away— who's probably forgotten you long ago.

Please tell me, I wondered to the cloudless sky as we listened to these songs day after day, why this bottom-feeder hired hand in the process of making steaks is so fascinating? Why not those who raise other livestock? Chicken farmers, for instance, I thought—the staple of my own Eastern Shore of Maryland. Then and there I made a resolution: somehow, someday, I would do for chicken farmers what Michael Martin Murphy and his kind have done for the cowboy. Both cowboys and chicken farmers are involved in getting animals on our table. But where, I asked despairingly, is the mystique of the chicken farmer? Why is America not as fascinated with them as it is with cowboys? Perhaps it's because chicken farmers typically sleep in a bed rather than out under the stars, and marry, and can hope to see their children grow up: all the things the cowboy, by definition a lonely out-of-money drifter, will never do. And they're the boss: we're celebrating the losers.

Deep Springs isn't a cowboy college; it's a subsidized farm with morning classes that can be scheduled between 8 and 11; students pay no tuition and in that sense "get a scholarship" (for which they work). I had it explained that it survives economically at all only because it's legally a college rather than a ranch, and gets tax breaks. No college, of course, survives without donations: it turns out that getting money is particularly hard for Deep Springs. Most funding sources nowadays, it seems, won't touch an all-male institution until it admits women, something forbidden by L. L. Nunn's Deed of Trust.

Co-education, it turned out, was a big topic among the students. Apparently the legal hurdles to overturning this weren't insurmountable, but the Board that oversaw the college, largely older ex-students, was against it. To me it seemed that bringing in women was disaster in the making: as it was, the students assured me, almost proudly, that they had no privacy at all. "You go in doors without knocking," one told me. "The agreement is you're not surprised by anything you see. Like masturbation. Or anything."

I decided I was too jealous of my privacy, or perhaps just too old, to find this appealing, and wondered how it would work with women. Would the Admissions Committee make half the class female and half male? Or would it do gender-blind admissions that might let in, say, two women out of 15, or 12? Would the women have to play at being "one of the guys" to fit in? What of the inevitable pairings (of course not zero even in an all-male institution)? How would you deal with the animosity that competition of two or more men for the same woman (or the reverse) in such tight quarters would engender? Where would the man and the woman go to get privacy? Where would either go when, inevitably, it was over? This was a place where everybody, I quickly found out, knew everything about everybody. Sexual relationships require some of the buffer zones of the adult world to work out. Deep Springs is not, in this sense, an adult world. Instead it seems like a Neverland of 19-year-old boys.

But not for that reason a happy place. One told me Deep Springers "spend the first year being unhappy at being there and the second year thinking about leaving"—apparently with mixed feelings. To a degree, they clearly were attached to it: after all, past high school, it's all most of them had known. As a result, perhaps, the common thread I heard among the students about to leave was a mixture of fear of the world outside and condescension: "Things will never be this intense," lamented one. "I wonder if classes at [the Ivy-league university he was going to] will be up to our standards?" said another. I, who had so recently come from the vast intellectual candy store of the world outside Deep Springs, with its museum exhibitions, its classic films, its lectures, its concerts, and its libraries, could only listen in perplexity. Do they have any idea what's *out* there? I wondered.

One Deep Springer, bound for an Ivy, said one evening that he'd only truly been happy working down in the garden. I'd seen him down there, one day when I went to find my sons, happily following the foreman's daughters across the fields. In the garden lay two of my students, one on each side of a long narrow hillock, like Gullivers among Lilliputians, picking tiny weeds out with their fingertips. Where they had plucked was a beautiful swath of brown earth with two perfectly spaced, tiny carrot plants set every three or four inches, their lacy tops green against the intense of the suddenly-uncovered brown. Where they hadn't plucked, the earth was invisible for the thicket of tiny weeds all but occluding the carrots the pair of giants sprawled on the ground above them had yet to uncover. As the hours passed, the six-inch-wide runner of brown soil unrolled down the hillock, propelled by their fingers: pinch, pinch, pinch, hundreds of tiny weeds to uncover a few tender carrots, and all afternoon to do it. Is this pitiful or inspiring?

300 Head
One day I broached again the subject of economic viability of the ranch with the farmer, the one with the big "guns" and the tattoos. The ranch has about 300 head of cattle. I asked if these made the ranch economically viable. He laughed. "Not at all," he said. It seems that to be economically feasible, it would have to have more cattle than it has, 500 rather than 300, but having that many would require more grazing area than the BLM, the Bureau of Land Management—that controls huge chunks of this part of the world—is willing to give the college. "Doesn't the fact that the student labor is free help the ranch financially?" I asked. He snorted. "We could hire migrants for not much money who'd do the jobs a lot better," he said. "These guys don't know what they're doing." The point seems to be to learn by doing; you're not trying to get anywhere, just be very intense about the journey.

One day, sitting in our seminar room in the main building where all classes take place (there are two seminar rooms; classes are staggered across the morning) at a seat with a view down the lane that I always took in order to remind myself that the world outside existed, one of the students, whose job was to take care of the irrigation pipes, admitted he was glad the pipes broke a lot. "It gives you more problems to solve," he said. "Hmm," I said. "Most people would wish for the pipes not to break so you could go on to something else." I hazarded the guess that the technology of the ranch was perhaps 1950s. "No," he said. "1970s." Why not 21st century, I wondered? Was this some sort of Amish doctrinal thing: no zippers on pants, only buttons? Why stop time at this particular point, except to make constraints?

A first-year student, this irrigation guy was on leave from an Ivy-level university to which he would ultimately return, where he went because, as he told me, he "hadn't gotten into Deep Springs the first time." He re-applied and got in. As we left the college at the end of the seven weeks he said: "I'm ready to leave Deep Springs. Only not yet." Getting in or not getting in getting in seems to be about whether you "click" with the other 19-year-olds on the committee when you come to visit, in the dead of winter, to see the college at its most isolated and least inviting. If you're not prepared to subsume your personality to the whole, you're not the right kind of person to begin with: they're taking the most compatible applicants, not necessarily the best.

Deep Springs College, clearly, wasn't about getting the crops irrigated, or the cows branded, or the pigs fed (there were pigs, horses, and chickens). It was about coming to terms with the fact that all this had to be done, and dealing with the inevitable problems in doing it. If the college were in New York City, the students would spend time fixing the subways. Or maybe not: there accidents would have consequences, and a screw-up on the subway would mean lives were endangered. Here, the students had safety nets that someone truly dependent on what he grew might not have. One day I asked if the eggs we were eating were Deep Springs eggs. "Nah," said one of the students. "A bobcat got into the hen house and wiped out the egg-layers." You keep chickens as a learning experience, but if a bobcat wipes them out, you go to the store like everyone else.

Upside-down T
At the end of the lane the trees stop, and I pass out under the wooden gate with the upside-down T at its top: this is the end of Deep Springs College property. When I asked what the upside-down T means, I got several answers. The one I think is true is that it was the sign of the ranch—its brand for cattle, among other things—when Lucien L. Nunn bought this ranch in 1917 and started Deep Springs College. I'm told that some people say it's the two "L"s of L.L. Nunn, one turned backwards. If it was the sign of the ranch before the college was started, this seems unlikely, but it may be why he kept it.

Nunn's money came from founding the Telluride Power Company in Colorado; he also endowed something called the Telluride Association, which runs living accommodations at two universities, and has, I was surprised to learn, a somewhat testy relationship with its "Nunnian" (the adjective is in local circulation) counterpart, Deep Springs College.

Unless Nunn kept the upside-down T just because he didn't want to re-brand the cattle. The ranch, I heard, was originally a cattle provider for a mining town over the Gilbert Pass and into Nevada, called Palmetto. We passed it the day we arrived at Deep Springs, and stopped to take pictures. Now it's something less than a ghost town, only a few stone walls by the side of the road. When it failed the ranch was sold. The inhabitants called it Palmetto because they thought, incorrectly, the local Joshua trees were related to the South Carolina palmetto from back home. Joshua trees are desert vegetation, all trunk and a few spiky crowns of leaves. Passers-through in the endless Nevada valleys see them sticking up at intervals in strange curves, like spears thrown at random by the gods that have begun to sag and melt in the sun, but have somehow taken root and put off runty green shoots.

The cattle brand and the gate on the dirt road leading out to 168, where I'm on my morning run, aren't the only places where I've seen the upside-down T. There are buckles with the upside-down T for sale in the main building, in an unmanned storage room: honor system for payment, here as everywhere. My favorite object for sale in this storeroom was a bright red T-shirt with silhouettes of L. L. Nunn, whose picture is in the buildings in a pose with his hand on the edge of his chair, and Lenin. On the front it says: "There were two social utopias founded in 1917." The back says: "One survived." This raised again the question that I tried to answer for seven weeks: How like Lenin was Nunn? Is Deep Springs a revolutionary institution or the escape of Luddites? Is it innovative, as the writer for the *New York Times* quoted on the brochure seemed to think, or the reverse? Does it spur its students to development? Or merely feed their 19-year-old sense that the world revolves around them?

There's also a much larger upside-down T laid into the linoleum tiles of the floor in the BH (there's a picture of L.L. Nunn over the fireplace). My sons loved being able to go themselves next door to the BH and help themselves at all hours to the left-over desserts that were put out for students to come and nosh; the early risers would sometimes just go into the kitchen and fry themselves some eggs. The cook, Priscilla, who explained she was really Northwest Indian but had been "adopted by white people" when a baby, made hearty ranch fare: she had been a ranch cook for most of her adult life. She arrived early—I usually saw her on my pre-dawn run, driving down the dusty lane from her house, one of a cluster of three that sat by the road, and were the only other structures in the valley besides the ranch and college buildings. Priscilla's breakfasts set the tone for the rest of the day in terms of nutrition and fat content: bacon, fried eggs (sunny-side-up), and pancakes made from white flour. Syrup wasn't maple, it was Aunt Jemima, corn syrup in huge gallon-sized plastic bottles. Despite the runs and realizing that I simply had to say "no" to much of the food in the BH and supplement at home (home was one building over in the circle of structures that constitutes the college) I gained five pounds during my seven weeks at Deep Springs.

Weight room

Other kinds of exercise also failed to keep the weight off. An ardent weight room junkie with access to the hardcore varsity athlete gym at the Naval Academy, my home institution, I made do at Deep Springs with a one-step-above-home weight room in the basement of the main building. The first day I went in it, I had to clear away the cobwebs from the doors (there is no cleaning staff at Deep Springs; one student's job is to mow the lawns, but this was done intermittently, and as far as I can determine, nobody ever pushes a vacuum cleaner in the buildings). When I finally found the light switch, it illuminated dumbbells of various sizes left off the rack and strewn all over the floor, a towel in a heap, various running shorts and socks dropped on the floor and thrown in corners, a couch with the cushions in a pile, a box of microwave popcorn packets, all expired, a wall full of dead or outdated computer equipment, several handfuls of long-play records cascading to the floor, and the door into a secondary laundry room. Before I could use the weights, I had to do some rudimentary housekeeping both for basic hygiene and to keep from tripping over all the junk.

Supplementing the BH wasn't easy. The closest supermarket was in Bishop, an hour's drive over the Westgard Pass and 15 miles north on 395, the highway that goes up the backside of the Sierras, and down to Los Angeles. Angelinos know 395, if it all, because it leads to the ski area of Mammoth Springs, a bit further north than Bishop, the town closest to Deep Springs. We took to going more and more often to Bishop as the weeks passed and came to feel more and more constrained at Deep Springs. Or as the land-line telephones failed. The computers, though usually reliable, were glacially slow. Half a minute ticked agonizingly by before each screen popped up; I hated watching the squares at the bottom fill in one by one from left to right. This computer slowness was especially bad in that my wife was trying to keep her hand on the tiller of her non-profit for a few hours a day, and spent hours on the land-line telephones. But when there was a problem with those, her life was disrupted. Sometimes she would take the boys and hit the road for Bishop, which boasted cell phone reception, as well as a park, a library, a pond, and spectacular views of the snow-capped Sierras.

Off the weight room was a sort of basement storage room with a hodge-podge of boxes, junk, furniture with missing legs, and a sheet tied from one set of ceiling beams to another. A hand-written sign at the door said: "Please do not touch ANYTHING." It was signed by a young man who later came to my door asking if I'd teach him an independent study course in Kafka. One day, I asked him about the sign: "Yeah," he said. "I should take that down. I was using that for a painting studio last term." I'd bet the sign is still there, and he's gone. He was one of the dairy boys, who let me and my sons milk the two milk cows with the other dairy boy for the 4:30 pm milking—I was never up for the 4:30 a.m. milking.

One day I visited the dairy barn at 4:30 p.m. My sons were across the dusty road at the tire swing under the trees. The dairy boys had killed a rattlesnake under the tire swing the second day we were at the ranch by throwing a nail-studded board over it while it lashed impotently and then cutting it in half with a shovel. Owen was riveted, and later on I came back and cut off the rattles and the head. I didn't have any rubbing alcohol and the college had no formaldehyde, so I put them both in mouthwash, which turned the rattles permanently green. To see what reaction I'd get, I repeated to the Kafka guy what another student had said: "We were the guys who got picked on in high school." He wasn't pleased. "I did all right for myself in high school," he said briefly, dragging on a cow's teat. "But I can see their point." He was also very informative about milking. He said his forearms began to hurt after the first half hour, and explained to me that you had to squeeze the teat half-closed with your thumb and index finger (otherwise the milk went back up into the cow, which was painful) and ripple your fingers closed down from that, in a kind of wave-like squeeze. He let me change places with him on the upside-down plastic milk crate, I did as he said, and it worked.

One day he came to class with his arms covered in dried blood. "What happened to you?" I asked. He looked down, clearly unsure what I meant. Then he saw the blood. "Oh," he said. "That's not human blood." He had just come from slaughtering the cow. The ranch foreman shot the cow and the students slit its throat and went from there. First milk a cow, then slaughter another one, grab some breakfast, then come to class, your arms covered in blood, to talk about *The Trial.* This probably seems intriguing to people on the outside; to me it seemed to lack clear purpose. Not to mention having a downside: Deep Springs students tend not to throw themselves on the material, but wait for the professor to tell them what they should note. No wonder, I thought: they're worn out. And I wonder what they learn from slaughtering a cow? That somebody has to do it? That it's messy business? That the little people who usually do all our dirty work shouldn't be underestimated? That life requires the sacrifice of life?

The beef in the BH came from the slaughtered cows. It was always tough and tended to be served as great hunks of meat that we had to saw at with a huge knife in the cafeteria line, the hunks identifiable as legs or thighs. One day the student I usually saw about the time I left for my run, rattling down the dirt road from a feed run in one of the farm's pick-ups, told me he'd fed the cow we were hacking apart. He'd fed it, the Kafka guy had cut it up, and Priscilla had cooked it. And here we were eating it. It was a very short food chain. The feeder guy, the one in the pick-up, was a vegetarian, as were a number of the students: there was usually a tofu variant of the main course sitting next to it, identified in magic marker written right on the metal rim that the tray went into. One day the guns-and-tattoos farmer, serving himself spaghetti sauce next to me, exploded in self-derisive laughter. "Jeez," he said. "I got the *vegetarian* one. Where's the one with the *meat*?"

Gossip

It was in the BH too that I was suddenly able to put my finger on what was so strange about the students socially. I was waiting in line for food when suddenly a cheery voice said, "Hi, and welcome! My name is Debby. Are you the new professor?" I had turned after the "Hi" and was smiling; we introduced ourselves and chatted. I got out of the line—only a few people long, in any case—to continue the conversation: her husband Les was in charge of the physical plant—fixed what went wrong with the houses, and so on. Debbie said they'd spent two years in Bosnia as missionaries. It turned out Les had been the minister at a church in Bishop; this was his retirement job.

What was so striking about this first interaction with Debbie was how normal it was for the world outside, yet how abnormal for Deep Springs. An outstretched hand, someone making introductions, following-up comments, some polite small-talk; it's the way people in the outside world acknowledge the distance between individuals: we go out of our way to bridge it. It's actually a sign of respect, because it says: I know you're not me, and have your own world. I'm offering mine; let's talk. Deep Springers, by contrast, would walk a foot away from me with their trays, their heads down to avoid acknowledging me. Nor were they any better with each other. They'd sit with each other with no greasing of the skids, no "may I sit here?," not even the universal male "Hey" or the more minimal slight lifting of the chin. Just bang, put down tray. And enter the same stream of common jokes and references they'd exited a few hours before at the last mealtime.

Fine, I thought, they're guys, and they know each other. No frills. Still, it's not more intimate to pretend that other people aren't other people; it's presumptuous, not to mention wrong. And solipsistic too: it assumes that other people are an extension of yourself. In the social world, you begin by noting the obvious fact that other people are different than you, then you go from there. Here, the assumption seemed to be that everyone would be the same. And perhaps they were right in making that assumption: they'd chosen each other, after all, and had to live with each other 24/7.

I made the effort at the beginning to sit with them, but found I was ignored unless I was willing to try and enter into this rushing stream of gossip and trivia. I noted that the young long-term faculty members seemed to have decided that the only way to beat 'em was to join 'em (or perhaps didn't even think in these terms): they chattered away with the students they sat with. Other people noted this too. The French camera crew, the students said jokingly at dinner before the men walked up to the table, had asked them to talk about their Wittgenstein papers while they were milking the cows. The silence or gossip that was their actual mode of communicating with each other wasn't telegenic or interesting enough.

Heating

The students live, in theory, two to a room in the dormitory where the dog got up to join me on my runs. But they told me that the heat doesn't work in half the building, and in winter the cold half ends up bunking with the hot half: in fact the hot half isn't even uniformly hot, with the place where the heat comes in the hottest and dropping off from there. The problems with the dormitory building had, apparently, been going on since its construction, which was only a decade ago. "Why don't you get the heat fixed?" I asked. The answers varied, but the common thread was that the system itself was outmoded; it made as much sense to install a new system, which hadn't yet been decided on (or was too expensive), as it did to fix the old. But it seemed the problems were those of the installer/designer. "Can't you hunt him down and make him fix it?" I asked. I was either asking the wrong people, or this fell into the category of being glad when the irrigation pipes broke because that made more problems to cope with.

This discussion gave me the information that before ten years ago, there was no dormitory at all. That part of the circle of buildings was empty. The dormitory was in the area of the main building, now the library, that itself had been renovated at the same time the dormitory was (apparently) so badly constructed. "It was really disgusting," said the student. (If a Deep Springer tells you the living conditions are "disgusting," you listen.) "At least that's what we hear," he went on. "Holes in the walls, rickety bunk beds, a real mess." Now the shelves with books filled the area; I found a *Gesamtausgabe* of Kafka's works in German to teach my impromptu Kafka class, and my guy—who subsequently brought a buddy, one of the four who stuck around for my other course— scrounged English-language versions of the texts: we started with what they had, and they express-ordered from Amazon.

There is no bookstore here at Deep Springs, and the library seems merely a holding-place for unread books. I'd gone to some trouble to send a stack of my own books months before I arrived: I remembered, when I was in college, feeling intense curiosity about the professor's world-view. Why should I wait to have it given me a spoonful at a time when I could go right to the shelf and find what it was in a couple of hours of reading? Apparently Deep Springers felt no such curiosity, or their bruising schedule of other commitments didn't allow them to satisfy that curiosity if they felt it. One day I needed to refer to one of my own books; I went to the catalogue to find them. Twenty minutes later, after searching with the aid of three different people (no one is on duty in the library; students don't even check books out—they just take them), I found the stack I'd sent more than six months before, in a dusty pile with scores of other dusty books "to be filed."

Speech Night

Les, the retired minister, also did duty as the speech coach. One night a week was "Speech Night." During the semester, it was a graded course; Les coached them; he told me he'd read their speeches (written out) beforehand and wouldn't let them get up if the speeches didn't make sense. He also made them stand up straight and wear a tie. I was delighted; at the Naval Academy much (properly) is made of standing up straight; I live in a suit and tie, and of course in a speech, projection is all.

I could only think that they'd slacked off since Les had things under control, and in any case now, in this spring term, the speeches weren't graded. Most speeches I heard during the handful of times I went in seven weeks were hard-to-follow stream-of-consciousness flows delivered with lots of mumbles by a young man looking down at and clutching a lectern. One was the agonizing attempt to wrest some sense from one of L.L. Nunn's enigmatic letters, printed with the Deed of Trust in a booklet I took to calling "The Little Gray Book"— none of them apparently understood the allusion to Mao Zedong. It spoke in passing of "largeness of heart"—this student's speech was the attempt to explicate this phrase with all the seriousness of a Talmudic exegete. Another speech was about the young man's experiences in a high school play, where he had to play a gay man: though most people assume he is gay, he noted soberly, "I am in fact heterosexual."

Even the more ready-for-prime-time students tripped over the generous helping of "like"s that they inserted—that is, that they like inserted—into their like sentences. Clearly living for months on end with no living beings other than the same guys and the cows (or chickens, if you were an egg boy) did little for the ability of introverted teenagers to interface with the adult world. This was a Neverland of 19-year-old boys—which is not to say their wet dream. Drugs and alcohol are prohibited, and if there's sex going on, it had better be kept quiet.

For all Deep Springers say that their isolated valley is magic ("the desert has a voice"—L.L. Nunn), they don't seem to be able to articulate why, except that it's what they've been looking at for months, or years. At one Speech Night a student spoke at rambling length of the fact that when his girlfriend came to visit (permitted after term was over) and asked him to show her some of his favorite places in the valley, he was rueful that he was unable to name any. It all seemed so intensely *there*, I gathered, and yet he'd never had time to visit any place, the time had gone. That was the tenor of what I heard over and over: it was all so intense, they were so tired, it had to make sense, L.L. Nunn's vision had to be respected—but what was the vision? What sense did it make? To what purpose all this intensity? They don't seem to be getting answers.

Fashion
I never had the courage to go inside the dormitory. Seeing the unpoliced areas of the main building was discouraging enough, and I knew that no one ever cleaned there either. Still, I've made my mark on the dormitory: I left a sweater for the "bone pile," one I'd inadvertently shrunk a size in the dryer. The "bone pile," they had told me, was the collection of commonly-owned clothes from which most of the students borrowed so as not to run around naked. One guy showed up day after day in a zip-up jacket I complimented him on: "Bone

pile," he said. The others rolled in wearing whatever they'd worn in the fields: a sweat shirt with holes, a ragged plaid shirt.

I discovered that this clothing style wasn't merely the result of carelessness, or having their attention focused elsewhere: it was a conscious statement. One student spoke slightingly of a chain-link bracelet another student had the temerity to wear: jewelry, it seemed, wasn't part of the Deep Springs aesthetic. And when we got to *The Tale of Genji*, which I'd excerpted for class purposes, they were scornful of the preoccupations of the eleventh-century Japanese characters with clothing, nuance of voice, appearance of handwriting, and adherence to social rules. They, at least in their own minds, were beyond that.

How could I show them they hadn't transcended clothing? This was a world where clothing had its own involuted set of rules as absolute as those in *Genji*. I tried showing up several days in a row wearing a tie, sitting opposite students in their bone pile clothes and dirty t-shirts. But the mental effort it took to teach four unshaven boys in communal hand-me-down sweat shirts was too great for me in a suit and tie. For a day or two I went to the opposite extreme, going unshaven to class in a t-shirt. But then I drew back from the brink and cleaned up, if not up to anything like the suit-and-tie standards I observe in my home institution, the Naval Academy. In their mind their rigid codes of dress were no codes at all, perhaps because nobody ever questioned them and here they were in their own little world, a world that constricted me more and more as the weeks went on.

The pictures in the one-building "museum" next to the main building showed young men with short hair and ties from the 1950s and 60s: apparently it had taken the Great Cultural Divide of 1968 to take this institution not only back to the same level as other schools—where students arrive in class in flip-flops, their baseball caps backwards on their heads—but to the level of farm laborers, or rather, upper-middle-class kids, largely from California or Massachusetts, acting out their pose of rebellion against the world that, after all, allows them their two years playing farm hands and their transfer to a prestigious university after that. Take *that*, you silly world!

I tried to stifle my impatience with them by reminding myself that I too had once been as full of myself as they, fully as self-righteous. I even tried to explain to them that the phase they were in wasn't the last they would go through in their lives—and that the reason I knew was that I'd been like them, once; that they were young and that there was another way of looking at the world. It turned out this was unwelcome news, or worse, patronizing: the notion that the whole world wouldn't take them at their own valuation was clearly something they'd never confronted before.

Philosophical Investigations

This term, there were courses in Desert Ecology, Wittgenstein's "Philosophical Investigations" ("of course they don't have any background," one of the two men teaching this course told me, "so we spend half the class just lecturing"), and mine, called "Eastern Classics" and mostly focused on some themes in English re-tellings of the two great Sanskrit epics, the *Mahabharata* and the *Ramayana*. Deep Springers, who stay only two years, leave with bits and pieces, unconnected dots, core samples but nothing in between. They don't do the fill-in on their own, because they're so busy doing other things. One day I mentioned "Aristotle's theory of tragedy" in passing to a class of students at the end of their second year and got blank stares: nobody had taught a course in that, so they had no idea what I was talking about.

It took me a while to realize that this "start every course from zero so they can take a taste of a lot of things" approach works best with what I came to call "T-shirt authors": nineteenth and twentieth-century writers producing individual works for a world quite like theirs, the kind of authors that Barnes and Noble puts on bags and shirts—Kafka, whom I did end up teaching, or Virginia Woolf, or Mark Twain. They don't have the context or background for anything but congenial works like these that came from their own world, the modern industrialized one. Probably for that reason, a New Critical "text-based" approach is presupposed: the text can be picked up and put down between labor and meals, and the point is the process of intense analysis of what's on the page, not a striving for anything larger.

Thus it also took me a while to realize they were frustrated by the nature of the books I'd chosen. They didn't seem to like it when I told them that the particular version of the *Ramayana* we're dealing with isn't any more authentic than any other: where's textuality now? They were waiting for me to talk about the words on the page, analyze the particular story on page 23 (which may well be an invention or embellishment of the American translator, who, the University of California Press book we were using noted, didn't even read Sanskrit). I think they thought me insubstantial: it's true that with more recent texts we can limit, and discuss, the variations, and propose something more like a "definitive text." Not so for older ones, or those from other traditions: I realized this concept itself was foreign to them.

Still, perhaps as a result of the fact that class is sandwiched in between hard physical labor on broken pipes, they concentrate intensely on what they're given, with a dogged concentration to detail that can be self-defeating. They seemed to think that the fact of their having seen something made it important. I found the students in my class all referring to the same critical essay that they'd read in a course the term before. I'd never heard of it; they seemed to think it was some kind of touchstone, rather than merely the one the professor had provided: "Critical essays are a dime a dozen," I told them. "You have to ask if it's useful." No one could tell me why it might be.

I thought I was doing them a favor by helping them at least pose the questions. I had started my class with a text that is usually included in the *Mahabharata*, the *Baghavad-Gita*. It's a conversation between Arjuna, one of the protagonists of the epic about a war between two branches of the same family, and his charioteer, who is the god Krishna, an avatar of Vishnu. The question the text raises is: How do I as an individual fit into the larger context of society? Arjuna, specifically, doesn't want to go to war against his relatives. Krishna tells him it's his duty: Arjuna is a warrior, and what warriors do is fight. Only you have to do what you do without regard to (positive) consequences—or negative either. Only this, according to Krishna, is pure.

I started with this because I thought it self-evident that people at this college, so isolated, so different, yet with its mandate of "service," had to be wondering how they would go on to serve the larger polity. I tried to get them to make the connection between the questions asked in the *Gita* and Deep Springs College. What duty do we owe to the collective? What if this clashes with our duty to ourselves—and what is this duty? They sat and looked at me. Why wasn't I explicating the text? And was I questioning their college? What right had I to do that? My job was to accommodate myself to the group, as they were doing.

Then the students started to disappear from class. One student left after asking me over dinner in the BH, What did the *Gita* have to say to a pacifist since it was just about duty for warriors? I began to stammer, certain that the question couldn't be as stupid as it seemed, then warmed up as I explained that it was about anyone's duty, this happened to be warriors, and so on. The next day he dropped the course, which at Deep Springs simply meant not showing up any more. I pressed on.

At the end of the second week, the letter arrived.

That weekend we'd gone on a long trip. I was tired when I got back but swung by the main building next door to see if we had any mail. We did. I also opened an envelope-less letter beginning Dear Bruce (everyone here is addressed by his or her first name, in a pretense of egalitarianism), and signed by the (student) chair of the curriculum committee that had hired me. He was in my class, still—but not all the committee members were. He "wanted to share some concerns of the committee about my class." I stood there in the silent mail room of the deserted main building not believing what I was reading. There in black and white, late at night with my other mail, I discovered that the students found offensive my attitude toward Deep Springs—questioning its presuppositions, apparently (there was no acknowledgment of the fact I'd come 3,000 miles losing money and uprooted my family because I thought the idea of the place was intriguing), were confused about whether the things I said were what they were to believe or merely trying to get them to react (what most people understand as the "Socratic method"), and asked that I focus on "the text" (this in a course devoted to thousands-of-year-old multi-version accretions that we were reading in English re-tellings by someone who couldn't read Sanskrit: they wanted sentences and paragraphs to refer to, like the classic Modernist texts). Most appalling to me was that my students had taken their grievances—which seemed to leave no aspect of my class, my attempts to engage them, or my attempts to remind them that they had to figure things out, unscathed and uncritiqued—to a committee, discussed me behind my back with people who didn't know me, and delivered an official indictment slipped into my box with my personal mail to be read on my private time.

Were they really so unaware how incredibly bizarre their little world was? They were free to knock on my door at any time, they showed up in dirty t-shirts, and addressed me as "Bruce." This suggested openness and informality. Yet they hadn't asked me, informally, why I was doing what I was doing, or brought up uncertainties when they saw me in class. Instead, an official oversight body, not all of whom were my students, had met behind closed doors to air their uncertainties, their incomprehension, their grievances, which they funneled through a representative who had written it all down in black and white and condensed it into a very formal written missive from an official body starting "Dear Bruce"—that I then read on my private time. Were public and private really the same to them? Perhaps they melded here at Deep Springs, but had they no idea that someone from outside wouldn't see it that way? Did they even know there *was* an outside?

In class, I'd been saying that I once had been like them, but no longer was. Yet reading the letter, I wondered if I had in fact ever been like them. These 19-year-olds, fatigued by broken irrigation pipes and as a result of knock-down, drag-out meetings with other 19-year-olds, isolated on their farm in a desert valley with only each other to focus on, lacked—so it seemed to me—any shred of humility. At their age I, by contrast, had at least been acutely aware of what I lacked. I had been terrified that I wouldn't in fact end up having the originality or mental capacity to do all I'd wanted to do in the world of ideas. Unlike them, I'd been aware that there were other minds more developed than my own that would take me months, perhaps years, perhaps a lifetime to understand. My job was to understand adults, not demand that they fit the small hole I was allotting to them in my busy schedule.

Yet clearly they assumed there was only one measure: their own. They demanded not only of each other but also of adults that they be on a first-name basis, have no more to say than could be said in a class period or boiled down to something they could eat in a hurry, like a fast food sandwich handed out of a drive-in's window. Questioning their world wasn't wanted: maybe it was too frightening for them to think they were so isolated and unhappy for nothing. There was no sense that they had to fit into the world, rather than make the world fit them. Here the world did fit them: it was made in their image, after all.

The irony of my situation was thick. I am given to questioning the Naval Academy, my home institution in books like *Annapolis Autumn: Life, Death, and Literature at the U.S. Naval Academy*, among other places, and alienate some people in doing so. I hear: this is the way it is, it's *my* Naval Academy, and you're the outsider! In fact, though a civilian professor in a military institution, I've been at the Naval Academy for over two decades. At Deep Springs, I began by saying I was an outsider trying to figure things out—and I was held to account for this too. Apparently I should be emphasizing how much I was a member of the "community." But that clearly meant keeping my mouth shut, and sticking to an exegesis of L.L. Nunn's offhand and insubstantial pronouncements rather than asking whether they meant anything at all. I knew the largely right-wing military didn't like to be questioned; it was a shock to find an institution at the other end of the political spectrum equally closed to self-analysis.

I was angry with myself. I felt like a mature man with grown children who, "thinking with the wrong head," has committed the folly of marrying, in a second relationship, a much younger woman. It feels invigorating at first, but what he realizes with a sinking heart as the weeks go on is that he's a complete person, with a developed inner landscape, and she isn't. All she wants to do is shop, she doesn't get his jokes, and she finds opera "boring." Instead of feeling young, he only feels old, and miles away from the person he looks at over the table.

If I had been alone, without my family, I would have thrown the letter in the trash, packed my bags in half an hour, and then and there, pushing midnight, gotten in my car, driven the four hours through the night back to Las Vegas, and gotten a hotel until I could get a flight out. But I was trapped. This was a family adventure, and so I had to take this hit for the team. I said nothing about this letter to my wife, and passed a restless night.

That next morning, awakening finally from a few drugged and intermittent hours of sleep, I couldn't wait to show this letter to the president. I assumed he'd share my fury, my outrage. I turned out he'd suggested the committee write it. They were here to learn how to deal with their problems, after all, and writing a letter, he said, was better than merely dropping the course. I couldn't believe my ears, and said so. Deep Springs College, I thought incredulously, would have invited someone from 3,000 miles away on a salary that didn't even cover airfare, who'd sent his books to have them ignored, who had re-arranged his life and that of his family for two months, for the privilege of coming to teach, for *zero* students?

Most of us have heard the joke about Heaven being where the hotelkeepers are Swiss, the cooks French, the lovers Italian, the mechanics German, and the policemen English. The joke is the second half, which imagines Hell as the cooks English, the policemen German, the hotel-keepers Italian, and so on. A world run by such self-centered, defensive, smart, self-involved, and intense young men barely out of high school is clearly closer to the latter than the former. The difference between myself and them is that, at their age, I was happy to let, to so speak, the Swiss run the hotels and the English be the policemen: it left me free time to focus on myself without hurting anybody, engage on a voyage of self-discovery that was like entering a long convoluted tube whose end was in one direction only: ahead. No turning back, no short cuts. Just keep moving forward until finally you're spit out at the other end and look around you, wonderingly, suddenly able to focus on the other people who have been there all the time: O brave new world!

At Deep Springs they aren't allowed to follow out the journey of the self while the Swiss hotel-keepers keep the place clean and the English policemen keep them safe: they're asked to run the hotels too, and be the policemen, cooks—everything but lovers, it seems (and that may come, if coeducation ever arrives—something expressly forbidden by the Deed of Trust but devoutly hoped for, it seemed, by the students). As the guns and tattoos guy said, they're no good at any of it. But that's okay: in fact, it's the way things are meant to be. At Deep Springs, the wheel is re-invented ten times before breakfast, and the point seems to be a dogged belief that the labor of re-invention has to have a point, if only they could concentrate long enough to figure out what it is.

Writing it down

At the gate with the upside-T is a wooden box. Inside—I looked one day on my morning run—was a log book and a pencil. It was half-filled with random thoughts, apparently recorded here for posterity by passers-by. "What a gorgeous day!" "I'm getting really tired of Deep Springs!" This, I discovered, wasn't the only such "I just *have* to write it down" book at Deep Springs. One day we went down to the lower reservoir ("lower res"—pronounced "rez") with three dogs—there was a large dog that belonged to an absent student, looking like Carl in the picture books, my running dog and his nearly identical buddy/sibling—and Priscilla's granddaughter. The lower res is two large square artificial ponds surrounded by trees and full of migratory birds. "This is the only water for miles and miles," one of the students told me. The rushes twittered, the water was full of strands of algae. The Carl dog, whose real name was Magnus, paddled in the water; frogs jumped in. And Priscilla's granddaughter reached under her, took a board off a box, and pulled out the comment book: it was like the book at the gate. Thoughts, dates, some names, the pages turning over and showing the effects of damp and then dryness. It seemed so odd, the verbal recalcitrance of the students that had frustrated me in the classroom, combined with these odd notes to Nature, or to no one, tucked into hollows.

The upper res, up a pathway behind the main building, wasn't lush at all. It was a concrete holding tank with a pipe spewing fresh water. It was surrounded by a fence, broken in places, and decorated with broken chairs along the rim, and some of them at the bottom of the tank. The students go swimming in the upper res, but the one time I went in it was just to show I wasn't afraid of cold water. Besides, it was uninviting: I wouldn't go in at all until the students fished out some of the broken chairs that had found their way in to the bottom, where you could see them sticking up crazily from the concrete like shipwrecks: not knowing the depth, I wondered if my legs would brush them swimming. It all seemed vaguely threatening.

The sensation of going through the gate on my run and leaving the ranch behind was like coming out from under a canopy and into the bowl of the valley. The trees, planted by people for people, stopped. At the gate the irrigation stopped too, and so did the green, at least green by East Coat standards. In fact the desert was abloom, the result, the farm people told us, of the fact that it had snowed a lot the winter before and the snow pack melted slowly. The sand was dotted with fragile white flowers; up on the Westgard Pass were the scarlet spears of Indian Paintbrush, and all over the sagebrush and desert holly. To eyes used to nothing, this was apparently lush; to eyes such as mine still were, it still seemed gray.

The sun by this point on my run—I was almost out to Highway 168—was closer to rising, but was still held captive behind the bowl of the valley on the east. Opposite, over the Westgard Pass, the light of the rising sun illuminated a cushion of faint pink, hovering in the sky. I looked down to dodge a pothole, and also to look for snakes—I'd seen a rattler going about its business one day, and on other days, several of the harmless gopher snake that gets some degree of protection from predators by miming the rattler (the glass door to the BH was covered with pictures of these two snakes, with explanations about how to tell the difference). When I looked up, the second of inattention had been enough to let the pink cloud of light descend to the snow-capped ridge of the Sierra Nevadas visible beyond Deep Springs Valley, suddenly glowing with pink fire. A few more steps and the pink had dropped to the closer mountains defining the valley. The light was spreading, intensifying in what seemed like huge second-long increments, now sliding down the rock face. Before I was at the asphalt road, the sunlight was halfway down the ridge, each rock suddenly given individuality; shadows, in the strengthening light of the sun, turning from pink to gold. And within moments, the valley was a golden bowl shimmering with light and I a tiny speck moving along a line of highway within it. I breathed light, my eyes open but surrounded by the liquid that had, in a split second where the sun was no longer occluded by the mountain behind me, spilled over to hit the floor of the valley like a giant paint bomb covering its floor and welling up the sides of the mountains.

Fence

About halfway through my run, by now along Highway 168, the dog is trotting along the highway with me, his nails click-click-clicking. We're nearing the cattle guard that's my point for leaving the highway and running alongside the fence that leads back to the lake road. The whole valley is aglow with the by-now fully risen sun, and the ranch sticks up beyond the sagebrush, the trees by the fields in rows. The sudden green of the crops is startling even from this distance, a far-off patch against the unirrigated desert.

I am running along the fence where there is a sort of path for farm vehicles. I can see my own footprints prints from yesterday, or perhaps another day—except for a Memorial Day sprinkle, which left the locals aghast as it was so unusual("it's *never* rained on Memorial Day," the librarian in Bishop said flatly), there's been no rain here at Deep Springs, nor none expected. Sometimes the students run along this path; in fact it was one of them who suggested it, and I decided I liked it better than a comparable loop in the opposite direction, toward the Gilbert Pass rather than the Westgard. Crows sit on the fenceposts with the barbed-wire underneath, gleaming black in the early morning sun. Over to the right is the white of the lake, at the end of the valley—where we found arrowheads, and where the branding took place. It's too far away for me to see the corrals, and the cattle are grazing closer to the ranch. They've shut the blue gate down by the paddocks to keep the cows out; I'll have to climb over.

Deep Springs Lake itself is largely dry, though from natural dessication, its surface made of white crumbled salt; one day, I walked out to the point where the depressions my shoes were making were too deep for comfort, and turned around. But there is water flowing into it, from the deep springs from which the valley and the college take their name. Next to the lake, on the side of the mountain, you look for the cluster of trees and the trails of rushes leading down to the crumbled surface of white salt. Standing at its foot, listening to the sound of rushing water, watching it sheen the rocks and glisten among the plants is like the jungle of the "lower res," another world. The leaves are lush, and the air simply hums with insects and glistens with the sun on the wings of what seem like thousands of dragonflies. Birds swoop and twitter.

Yet a few feet away you're once again you're in the desert among the sagebrush, the cliff walls rise austere and gray around you, and the dusty road back to the ranch will kick up a plume of dust that from a distance looks like a tornado. Somewhere in the water, I've heard, are hundreds of the ugly black toads that live only here, in Deep Springs (a recent scientific article I found online says they've been introduced into a springs in Death Valley as well, and are also up at Antelope Springs on the other end of the valley, where the cowboys take the herd in the summer). In any case I left Deep Springs without ever having seen the toad.

In the wall of the mountain, visible from the spring, is the mouth of a small cave where, the students tell me, the Paiute Indians, whose baskets I've seen in the museum in the county seat of Independence, hid from the U.S. Cavalry that had come over the pass from the Owens Valley to rout them out. "What's in there?" I asked students. "Smoke on the walls and not much else," they said.

In the dust of the road alongside the fence are the tracks of animals. I can't tell what—they don't let the cattle graze here; perhaps they're from a bobcat like the one that got into the hen coop; they're too big for the mangy coyotes that skulk through the valley. Here in the uninhabited desert, the dirt keeps animal tracks for weeks, not just my running footprints. For weeks after Owen and I took a walk down to the cow barn with him dragging a stick to "make snake tracks" (this was shortly after he'd seen the rattler killed, and we'd put its head and rattles in mouthwash), large portions of the twisting line he left were visible, blotted out only by the rubber boots invariably worn by one of the dairy boys, and the flat tennis shoes worn by the other, or my own shoes, or the farm-mobile driven at breakneck speeds by the other irrigation guy, the one whose banging versions of Lizst made the piano in the main room shake ("I keep telling him he has to get some pianissimo," complained the itinerant piano teacher who came once a week from the Owens Dry Lake area—one week he was shaking his head about the dust storms in the lower end of the valley: "couldn't see a thing the dust was so thick," he sighed).

Finally I am at the end of the fence—measuring distance by fenceposts gives the run a feeling of normalcy that the lost-in-the-valley part did not—and turn left, at the sign that says, Deep Springs College Property. A right turn would bring me to the lake, about six miles out, with the spring and the corrals for cattle branding; a left goes back to the ranch, about a mile.

Here too is the dump. It's here at the end of the property, like the dump at the edges of every ranch in the Great Basin—as the huge depression between the Sierras and the Rockies is called. Driving in Nevada, you can see the property line of every ranch: far away is the main house, surrounded by the only visible real trees (not Joshua trees, actually a type of yucca plant) for miles around. You know where the end of the property is because of the pile of abandoned cars and refrigerators that stick up out of the desert. The land beyond is controlled by the BLM.

The Deep Springs dump, also at the edge of the college property, has its share of refrigerators and old cars. It's not so much a dump as an area of the desert strewn with large metal things. One of them looks like a cement mixer pointed at the sky. There's a pile of road signs, most pockmarked with bullet holes. One day I turned them over: High Desert Rig Runners, one said. Another had a picture of a truck going down a triangle with "7%" on the triangle, to warn vehicles (especially trucks) of a descent. White metal cabinets are here too, and dead cars. Boxes that have rotted away with the rusting parts for farm machinery fill in some of the spaces between the larger objects, and loops of rusted bailing wire in strange flattened whirls dot the sand.

On the right side of the dirt road, where only a few things have been dumped, or perhaps have simply migrated, sits a more recent reject, a broken institutional-style student's desk from, perhaps, 1970, trying for sleek but, by marrying this with wood-grain plastic, achieving only clunkiness. On it sits an electric typewriter, too like the one on which I typed my dissertation more than a quarter century ago for me to see it as anything but a piece of broken trash; perhaps to the eyes of the 19-year-olds it is already covered with the haze of nostalgia. Its electric cord trails over the side of the desk, and trails in the dust—as if the power for this abandoned object now comes from the air, or the desert itself. A waggish Deep Springer has inserted a piece of paper in the platen and arranged a chair in front, slightly ajar, as if an invisible person had just got up. Down close to the cattle gate are the cows, let loose to graze in this part of the valley. They watch me run closer, then all at once run off in a minor stampede into the sagebrush. Then, equally abruptly, they stop all at once, their heads all turned towards me, their eyes following me mistrustfully as I clamber over the gate and pick up my jog on the other side. I can leave the college property, but I'm still caught in the valley.

I'm heading back; class starts in an hour.

7
Running in Las Vegas

Early Sunday morning in Las Vegas, as on the Rambla in Barcelona, is for most people late Saturday night.

The sky was light, but the air still misted with gray. We were staying a block off the Strip—a hotel that, we learned, businessmen prefer because it's somehow less "Vegas," more low-key. Still, its lobby blinks and dings with slot machines, even at 5 a.m. when I walked through on the way outside to run, and anyone going through the sliding glass doors that walls off what later in the day, and the summer, will become 105 degree heat, is struck by the same smell of beer and stale cigars that fills every hotel in Las Vegas. It's the smell of Vegas, it seems, air-cooled but with undercurrents of something just under the barrier of nausea, as specific and stomach-churning as ammonia, only weakened to the point of toleration.

Next to the hotel was a vacant lot, surrounded by a chain-link fence, its dirt the same gray powder that begins at the end of the last housing development out at the extreme edge of Las Vegas, where we had visited with friends. An inch further than the fence around the last house is the desert obscured by the development: the drop-off is absolute, accomplished in a matter of micro-millimeters. And the vacant lot just off the most developed part of Las Vegas, the Strip, is a reminder that in any exposed area the desert comes back, the same gray powdery sand obscured by all these buildings. Of course because this vacant lot is an enclosed piece of desert in the city, rather than part of the wasteland all around Las Vegas, it's full of Vegas trash. Cans, a feather duster, a piece of what looks like a machine.

Plus the girlie cards. Lots of them, thrown on the gray sand, on the sidewalk, face-up, face down. Natasha, they say. Or Kim. No Sallys, or Marys. Picture on the front, contact information on the back. These have been thrown away, probably within seconds after having been handed out by touts on the street, and many have been walked on. They're the same girls that, in much larger blow-ups, grace the sides of the ubiquitous "Girls Who Want to Meet You" advertising trucks that circulate down the Strip and then back again, complete with large and easily readable phone numbers: perhaps you're meant to whip out your cell phone then and there and place an order. If the first truck (really a mobile sideways sandwich board) gets by without you copying or memorizing the number, there's likely to be another identical one just behind it, or when the next light turns green.

But the vacant lot is the exception: I'm in a world of lights and marquees from eateries, here on this side road that intersects the Strip. The air is gray, but the lights under the marquees are still burning bright. However now it's only under the overhang that they seem like sources of light; the bulbs on the facades of the buildings, now surrounded by the gray air of morning, have diminished, and every minute of strengthening light around them will reduce their reach even further, until they are nothing but glowing dots, like a dab of color in an Impressionist painting.

This bitter end of Saturday night, couples are still standing in a line for taxis. The males look like fraternity boys. They're not well dressed: shirt tails hanging out, beer bottle in their left hand, shorts. On their right arm is a girl, each of whom looks as if she has consulted the same book on "how to look hot" and have followed its rules to the letter, without really understanding. Or maybe they have understood; it's simply that men all want the same thing. All hair is long and shining, all dresses end at mid-thigh, all the heels are high and thin, all the backs of their feet are exposed, all straps are spaghetti. I move off the sidewalk into the street to avoid colliding with them and the somewhat tipsy men. The men seem to have more energy than the girls, laughing and making jokes to their buddies (the men are invariably in groups); the girls look somewhat faded, though they are smiling broadly.

Prostitution isn't actually legal here in Las Vegas, though you'd never know it from walking up the Strip in the evening. Officially the women are paid "companions," hanging around the men while they play the slots, or at the tables. What goes on later is apparently unrelated to this official function, and in any case famously "stays in Vegas." Yet clearly the conviction for running a prostitution ring in Washington, D.C. of the shopworn Debra Jean Palfry, and her subsequent suicide—which took place while we were in and around Nevada—was the result only of her location in staid Washington, D.C. Seen from the Strip, her defense that her girls were simply companions seems reasonable, or as reasonable as what goes on here in Vegas.

Paying girls for sex, rather than for "companionship," is, however, legal in the next county up, which explains why, driving north along the east side of Death Valley, on Highway 95, we see clusters of low dusty buildings off of side roads, in the middle of the sagebrush but connected to the highway by an unpaved access track: Bordello! one of them trumpets from a sign by the side of the highway—this is certainly truth in packaging. Others are more coy: one calls itself the Shady Lady Ranch, and the one at the corner of the yet smaller road we take to go over into California, on the north side of Death Valley and the Eureka Valley, has closed and is shuttered, so the tumbleweed reigns supreme in the parking lot. Now this has a neutral name, Johnson Farm or something similar. The parking lots of the ones closer to Vegas, the ones still open, are well stocked with big-rigs, their drivers inside giving the place some business.

The friends who live on the northern edge of Las Vegas, in that last development before the desert (where they ride their dune buggies, illegally as it turns out, since this kicks up dust—Dust Mitigation Area, read the somewhat perplexing signs, perplexing at least to me, so they have to explain that this simply means "Don't Ride Your Dune Buggy Here"), fill me in later: the girls from Los Angeles arrive in time for Friday night, disembarking at the airport already in their working gear, what I now see on the streets. I wonder if they wear running shoes into town, and then change, like the office workers back home in Washington, D.C.

At the end of the block, I turn right onto the Strip, and the girls thin out, perhaps because there is more room for them so they're diluted. Plus the light has strengthened, the street is wider; it seems odder to see them in their sexy-by-the-numbers dresses in broad daylight. Here there are sometimes pairs of girls, obviously getting off work, and the odd cluster of the guys, still with their beer-bottles, but already having paid off the girls. At this hour of the morning, or the late end of night, the lights are still flashing on the restaurants, and the slot machines I see working away inside are 24/7, but with the light strengthening they seem isolated data in a world with a lot of other things going on in it, not the center of attention.

Besides, aside from the bitter-enders straggling out on this border area between extremely late Sunday night and extremely early Sunday morning, there are simply fewer people here at this time of day than there will be in even a little while. Hours later, closer to 9 a.m., walking along with my family, I am conscious of perhaps as many as a dozen runners up and down the Strip in the course of a half an hour. Almost all are trim 30-something women, too old and too practical looking for hookers (aside from being out at the wrong time of day), lacking the lustrous sweeps of hair of the glamorous ones. They're in Lycra and Spandex, but their hair is practical and short, and they're running with friends. The hour is a decent one, before the real heat of the day kicks in but allowing them to sleep late: it's Sunday, after all. Now, all I see is a man or two, a typical stringy runner in a T-shirt: no glamour there either.

The sidewalks are mostly deserted here on the Strip itself, however, so I don't have to weave around people. Even the street is empty, so I could run there if I wanted to. This hour of the morning, except for the people finishing up old business on the side streets and inside, just isn't Las Vegas's finest moment. The buildings aren't so far gone as to be forlorn; for that we'd have to imagine a giant earthquake that would split them open and topple their upper floors, or the slow turning to semi-ruins as the result of time and the shifting of attention elsewhere that is imagined in Hubert Roberts's fantasies in the Louvre of the Grande Galerie in ruins, a painting that hangs in the very room imagined to be derelict, the roof broken in, and washerwomen doing their laundry exactly where we stand. They're just empty. Vegas is for gambling, shows, and girls, and aside from the people who literally never leave the slots for a week, this is not their time. It's like the diurnal version of "off-season" for a resort. Vegas has diurnal lulls, times when it drowses, or is simply unnoticed: the graph of use here would have to be made on the basis of a day, perhaps at most of a week, with the slight variations of seasons (Christmas and summer crushes).

Everything has a front, I was reminded in Barcelona, like our faces that point in one direction: we're so used to turning this to another face that we forget what we leave behind when we turn it. The temporal equivalent of a front is high season, or a time of day. The front of these buildings is partly temporal, the time of day when they come to life, get dressed, and are ready for action. Other things have temporal "fronts" too: the beach, that wakes into life near lunch and goes strong until close to sun-down, and this only in the extended summer season. And they have backs too: think of the quiet of a seaside boardwalk in the early morning: everyone has gone home, the breeze blows a piece of trash across the boards. Some of the people who have spent the night in the sand are stirring, ungluing themselves from each other, or brushing the sand from their body, awakening with the sun: a few seagulls caw overhead, or land on an abandoned piece of food. A theater aside from those few hours when it is waked to life, lit, filled, and put to use, is empty, a cavernous shell: these off hours predominate. Schools that sit empty in the summer have begun to schedule summer day camps in an effort to fill these off times, in their cases less than the "on" times.

Las Vegas isn't in ruins, and since the difference between high season and low season throughout the year isn't visible to the casual visitor, being trackable only in the takes of the casinos or the bookings of the hotels, the only variations are measured in hours. This is the time, my running hour, when people withdraw their attention. The lights blink, it seems, to no purpose; the fountains over at the Bellagio produce their flumes to only a few passers-by; the street lights change for only a few cars.

I'm close to the Venetian so I make that my first goal. The artificial light that makes the canals shine, especially under the bridges, hasn't yet been rendered impotent by the strengthening daylight. I read that the hotel's designer re-painted the blue several times, trying to get just the right color. I also read that he was pleased that his canals, unlike those in the real Venice, didn't stink. Because the canals here are much shallower than those in Venice, they're not dark on the bottom; they're this robin's egg blue someone is so proud of. And it's true the water doesn't stink, at least not of the garbage and pollution of Venice. This water is sterile, and smells of chlorine. I run up a ramp leading up to the entrance to the shopping arcade, closed and deserted, and the Rialto Bridge, from there to the loggia of St. Mark's Square that look down over the moored gondolas: I'm moving too fast for these structures, and even with no one about, feel that I'm going to run into a pillar. So I stop and walk. It's cool still; this is early May, and it isn't 6 a.m.

Riding a gondola at the Venetian in Las Vegas is like navigating a toy boat in a landscaped pool, or in a water park with a tubing loop, lined channels in the ground in which the same detoxified water full of hundreds of kids and a few overweight adults circulates around and around and around. Seen from above, at this hour of the morning, it seems pretty silly: an amusement ride, rather than a functional means of transport. It only ends up bringing you back to where you started anyway: the point is the voyage, not the goal.

But then again all of Las Vegas is about the voyage, not the goal. Indeed, it's so voyage-not-the-goal it's become its own goal, mapped out from the air as a tiny square in the middle of the desert in this vast valley: from an airplane there is nothing and nothing and nothing, and then suddenly Las Vegas. To a Baudrillard, in search of the hall of mirrors he took America to be, Vegas is like Disneyland: signification chasing a signifier.[19] To someone who comes here, however, for a weekend, it *is* the signifier: the rubric to be filled is "having a good time," and this is where you come to have it. It's already the exception to life that proves the rule.

Las Vegas is the place that's a "there" because there's no "there there," to echo Gertrude Stein about Oakland, California. It's beside the point to talk about how the hotel up the way, Paris Las Vegas—where you can't run because so much of it is inside, the Left Bank/Ile St-Louis stroll being a long corridor with a ceiling painted in not-quite-*trompe l'oeuil* blue sky and clouds (it's too shiny, for starters, and the vaulting of the ceiling is too obvious)—isn't Paris. So too it's silly to point out that the canals here are nothing but a large oddly-shaped shallow in-ground pool, as if the swimming pools in the housing developments of greater Las Vegas, or California, when seen from the air, intense blue dots, had been strung together—like the John Cheever short story "The Swimmer" about a man who swims across suburbia and gets surreally old doing so.

If you start with Paris, or Venice, you have to get Platonic on Paris Las Vegas or the Venetian, seeing these as shadows of the Ideal, or perhaps the shadows of the shadows. Or would that be the Venetian hotel and casino in Macau, itself a simulacrum of the Las Vegas instantiation? They're not fake Paris or Venice; they're real gambling hotels. Which means they're indoor spaces protected from the desert heat by big walls and with entrances to get you inside. The walls seen from outside aren't the point, nor the sidewalks and streets that get from one to the other.

Las Vegas is the female equivalent of a "male" city made with its parts evident, outdoors: it's all indoors, an inverted place. Like the DuPont synthetic material Dynel—for which the slogan in the 1950s was "it's not fake anything, it's real Dynel"—Las Vegas isn't profitably seen as fake anything. *Pace* Freud, women aren't just badly designed men. Even the "so bad it's good" view of Las Vegas of Robert Venturi's *Learning From Las Vegas* is as dated as post-Modernism in general.[20] Las Vegas isn't a city at all. It's the outdoors turned indoors. Las Vegas is an inverted world: all its functional parts are indoors, and the façades are meant to get you in. You aren't actually meant to be on the streets at all.

Island

The most fundamental fact about Las Vegas is that it's an island in the desert, like a raft in the ocean. The hotels are really covered space to make an air-conditioned world, like malls where people go walking in the morning, with various themes to keep them from being monotonous, or Montreal's "City Down Under" that links various snow-free passages and walkways to create an alternative space for winter living. Even the outsides of the buildings are determined by this fact. This being the desert, the greatest luxury is water. So you show it off, you build receptacles for it and you expose it to the air to evaporate: this is conspicuous consumption at its purest. Of course you have to put down cement so it doesn't immediately sink into the desert sand: that isn't artificial, it's a given. Thus, the claim to fame of the Bellagio across the street from where I run is its huge (artificial, of course) lake, and its nightly fountain show. And all the hotels have pools, which play a greater or smaller part in their self-presentation: greater at someplace like Mandalay Bay, which is a forest of tropical vegetation in keeping with its motif of the steamy jungles of Southeast Asia, smaller in the much more functional, city rooftop pool of the Westin, where we were staying.

What Las Vegas is burrowing against isn't the snow, as in Montreal, it's the heat and dryness. And the heat doesn't build up on the ground, but in the air. So it's enclosure we want, not depth. Hence the interior world of Las Vegas. My spot on the loggia of the Venetian looking down on the gondolas is as exterior as it gets and still remaining a real part of Las Vegas: the truly external areas, like the sidewalks, are nothing but ways to get to the enclosed areas. They're ugly, ill kept up, and at this hour of the morning, dotted only with drunks. I'm outside, but I'm still in the building, and about to leave Venice for the Roman Forum across the street—or rather, for the enclosed space of Caesar's Palace that I know about from a visit the day before, and that I don't visit running. One doesn't run in buildings, of course, and the inside, the lobby, is the "front" of the building, what they want you to see.

Las Vegas isn't set up to have you run up Las Vegas Boulevard, the Strip. It's set up to have you be in and around the hotel of your choice. You're allowed to go elsewhere to see a show, but basically you're supposed to pick a sub-world and stay within it. The more enclosed hotels, like the Mandalay Bay, become their own worlds, the only place outside of the airport its occupants see. That's Venturi's mistake: to see the city as a whole, as if from the outside. In fact the collection of all these insides, completed with façades, so that the inside begins as you emerge from the taxi, is not a cityscape. It's random, incidental: this may be what Las Vegas looks like to the runner, or the stroller, but the fact is, runners and strollers are beside the point in Las Vegas. Running from one façade to the next is much too fast, causes the reaction that this is like a whirlwind tour of something, Disneyland on steroids—and hence the simulacrum of a simulacrum: to get from one world destination to another you don't even have to travel to another part of the theme park; all you do is go next door.

In Paris Las Vegas the night before, Saturday night, we wandered and wandered, getting lost several times, looking for the way up the half-sized Eiffel Tower. One bit led to the next, our way blocked at every turn by banks of pinging, blinking, slot machines. I'm told that in the old days of the "one-armed bandits," with a lever you actually had to pull (that was the one arm) like a water-pump handle attached to the machine, people would feed the machines silver dollars, coated in graphite to allow easier insertion (a sort of lube-up); as a result after an hour or so they'd have hands coated in black, and gradually over an evening and into the wee hours the black would spread to their clothes, which they'd touched, and to their foreheads and mouths, which they'd wiped, like a fungus moving outward. Now everything is credit cards and there are no arms on the machines: it's sobering to think that someone somewhere designs them for a living. My favorite among those I examined was a slot machine with a DaVinci theme, with a handful of his most well-known paintings standing in for the classic fruit.

Finally we found the entrance to the Eiffel Tower, though it was closed, and the outdoors beckoned me like a lighthouse: somewhere out there, I knew, was air, and a sidewalk, and some way to get my bearings. Even so, two legs of the Eiffel Tower were inside the building, so apparently outside was already in; why go out? Meg had read that the hotels were purposely designed so as to be confusing; that way people wandered forever among the slot machines and never sought the air: they played more, and so lost more.

Minotaur

The architecture in Las Vegas is actually a series of mazes to catch people, endless insides. Certainly the previous night we had felt that some of them were mazes with no centers, not even a Minotaur. Or was the Minotaur of the MGM Grand its celebrated lion?

It's a sign of something (perhaps only my own ignorance) that I didn't even "get" why the MGM would have a lion (think of the movie logo in classic 40s movies; it roars, twice)—so far had this hotel-among-hotels strayed from its roots in the movies. I'm not even sure I knew why there was a golden lion, as large as a small building, outside on the corner. That's just the way it was, I suppose I thought: certainly the hotel itself does nothing to encourage people to think of movies: no stills of classic stars, no crank cameras on display. And perhaps I'm not the only person who simply assumes that of course the Grand, as most people called it, had a lion at the center of its maze, without asking why.

The Grand's lion didn't roar, as we discovered twenty minutes after trailing around lounges, restaurants, card tables, and the rows upon rows of blinking beepers. We had to ask twice where the lion was, then read the signs (they say "Lion Habitat," whatever a habitat is in this case), and move from area to area. It was worse than an airport, because this was completely inside, lit only by the blinks and stares of artificial lights. We'd get to a sort-of crossroads (only there were no right angles; area branched off from area, like a ballooning fungus) and had to negotiate the paths branching in various directions, curving around yet another bank of slot machines, another line of dealers, male and female, wearing bow ties and black vests, and perched behind tables where they spread out the cards, hour in and hour out. We went up, then down, around another whole bubble of restaurants, following signs to "Lion Habitat."

Finally we found it. The lion not only wasn't scary, it wasn't even awake. And its "habitat" made perfect sense in this turned inside-out world: a huge glass box. The lion was so oblivious to his surroundings that there was a man inside trying to invigorate him, apparently to make him worth the interest of all the families clustered around, many with children. The lion wasn't interested in the rubber ball attached to a rope that the man swung at him: he tried to be, it seemed—one paw reached out from where the lion was lying on his glass shelf in his glass cage and batted feebly, then retracted. The man himself had a big and very round gut, straining against a dark t-shirt, and no apparent defenses against the lion: the result was an impression of less than fierceness in the animal.

The real draw for the glass lion "habitat" was the tunnel, also of glass, into which people crowded—underneath the lion. Underneath, that is, the glass shelf on which the lion snoozed. Families—including mine, with wife and two boys—crowded into this narrow opening, like the entrance into a pyramid, to look up at the clear if somewhat blurred outline of the lion's backside, tail, and forequarters, making a print as they pressed against the now-much-touched glass. One Hispanic family held up a tiny girl with pigtails, her ears already sporting the requisite Hispanic just-after-birth girl's gold earrings—she reached out her hand and touched the glass that touches the lion, on the other side. The family was delighted, and went off into gales of laughter. It was stuffy in this tunnel, and people coming in or out have the frozen half-smiles of people negotiating their way out of a crowded elevator, something between "it's a nice day isn't it?" and "I'm so sorry to disturb you." This is what's at the center of the indoors: a sleepy lion and moues of regret from the too many people.

The limits of the Strip, like the city limits of Las Vegas, are easily reached. By the time I'm across from the Excalibur—with only Mandalay Bay between me and the end of the hotels—I'm at the end. I've passed New York New York with its Statue of Liberty and Coney Island roller-coaster, and see only the trash on the sidewalk: thus it's fitting that the Mandalay doesn't even try for a façade. You drive in a taxi past a Southeast Asian gate choked by tropical vegetation, and are within. Luxor, one hotel up, has an external pyramid and a laser show from its transparent tip, but it too is inside, with Abu Simbel-like colossi in the lobby. Still, there's no meaning in the alternation from New York to the Pharaohs to Camelot to Burma. Instead, the Strip is as if the side of a building has been torn away by the wrecking ball, and all the floors too, leaving to the viewer's eye the green wallpaper of one now-ripped-away apartment, the beige paint of another, the red stripes of a third, next to each other and outlined by the places the missing walls designed against what remains. This isn't supposed to make sense, and it doesn't: no more does the succession of maze-like interiors that is Las Vegas, when seen from the vantage point of a runner.

Bunkers

Yet there are streets in Las Vegas where things settle into coherence, the outside in which I run becoming a place again rather than merely the means to enter one of a series of unconnected insides. Now I'm running down the street with the Westin again, the part of town with the monorail that seems so inviting at first glance: a hotel concierge had told us it offered "fabulous views of hotel employee parking lots." And it's here that a sense of place emerges. For what line these streets, a block or two off the Strip, is the towering blank bunkers that enclose the insides. These at least are real with respect to the world around them, closing out what must be closed out: the heat and the desert.

The walls are like great castles that go down the mountainside to offer a view that no one inside ever sees: this is the purely functional part of the building, the parking lots which connect these to the real world, with the housing developments stretching out to the abrupt cut-off line with the desert. Here Las Vegas is a place, anchored in the desert, and what we see are the anchors, the great thick walls that keep out the heat and dryness, and create its interiors.

8
Running in Death Valley

The heat index in Death Valley in mid-May varies according to the time of day. It's the height of things, mid- to late afternoon, that gets calibrated—up to 120 degrees Fahrenheit in July and August. The hottest temperature ever recorded was at Furnace Creek Ranch, now a motel and resort with a golf course a few miles from the lowest point in the Americas, where we are staying: 134 Fahrenheit, and so hot that according to report, the birds fell from the trees.

In May it's perfectly tolerable in the morning, the running hours. I start looping around the roads within the ranch. Away from the motel-like accommodations, the hot springs pool, and the public buildings is the world of those who work the public buildings: trailers, small houses with a sense of something like permanence, a world that isn't forbidden to the tourists but simply off the path they'd take from the main entrance to the motel and back to the restaurant. I talked in the gift shop with one of the people who lives here: a middle-aged woman, she's alone, and works this resort until it gets really hot, then transfers, she explained, to the shop at Yellowstone. It's a life. Any place has its own normalcy, and this is the normalcy of Death Valley, with its televisions, its computers, its work hours—and not much else.

By the main entrance of Furnace Creek Ranch is the Borax Museum. It's a more buffed-up version of the not-ready-for-prime time museums I've visited in the weeks before, repositories of local memory that, back East (as even the people who have never been East say out here) tend to either not be made or disappear, where the usual story of pre-historic to post-Modernist rules the museum world. The story here begins in the mid-nineteenth century, and sometimes mere decades later.

One such is at the railroad junction in Laws, outside of Bishop: it's a collection of buildings built around the end of the line for a short-lived railroad going north-south down the Owens Valley. They make two "streets" up the sides of a grassy middle area where the most famous train is parked: a few of the buildings were actually associated, here, with the railroad; some of the buildings have been moved here from elsewhere (a dentist's office, a post office), and some are movie-set buildings from a Steve McQueen movie whose violence, later, made my wife and me abandon watching it back East after fifteen minutes. One of these was the Wells Fargo office in the movie, and still says "Wells Fargo Office." It's the building with rock samples and also, more endearing, musty showcases that give answers to the question, how do you display arrowheads? The answer seems to be, you make florettes of various sizes out of the whole ones and arrange the partial ones into rough mosaics of soaring eagles or coyotes baying at the moon: some of the arrowheads on the remnants of someone's long-ago collection mania have fallen off and lie in the bottom of their showcases.

The Borax Museum sees more tourists than the Laws Railroad Museum, and it's been to charm school. It's an old-time building on the other side of the street from the restaurants, but out back are the abandoned machinery pieces that I've discovered are part of many museums in this part of the world: the Inyo County museum in Independence, the county seat (Death Valley, the lowest spot in North America, is in Inyo County, as well as Mt. Whitney, the highest mountain in the continental U.S.) also has its parking lot of rusted wheels and pullers that roll and pull no more.

Seeing these once-functional things motionless and too large for their surroundings somewhat takes the punch out of a lot of back-East sculpture, the on-beyond-David Smith things of great wheels and arcs that fill up whole galleries. Back East after our California trip, for example, I went to an exposition of Martin Puryear's constructions as if versions of these abandoned machines whose interest, such as it is, is that he's changed the material to wood and they're inside, a whole room devoted to nothing but a single huge (20 feet high) wooden wheel and axle, somehow bereft of its second wheel and never functional. Do these people think we're so far from our mechanical past that they have to make simulacra to have us notice the melancholy of the abandoned machine? Here in Death Valley we aren't: up the road is the abandoned Borax mine, with some of the machinery out front, and indeed all of Eastern California and Nevada is dotted with abandoned machinery at the edge of the property like the Deep Springs dump.

In this general-store-like building (a sign says it was moved here from elsewhere), you first enter the gift shop—a good sign that it's tourist-savvy. The exhibits are in the same space, and tell the story of the first people trying to cross Death Valley on their way to what they hoped were riches in the California gold rush of 1849. Death Valley turned out to be a trap from which they exited only by going south, and sending some members of their party for help. Many died; this gave the valley its name. Mineralogical showcases explain the nature and use of "Twenty Mule-Team Borax," and pictures explain the 20-mule-teams that pulled it across the mountains. One of the more interesting facts these impart is that the team was actually only 18 mules; they needed two horses on the sides for intelligence. The curves over the mountains required a sort of over-shoot by the team and then making an angle backwards: this was a skill the mules had to learn.

Borax for someone who grew up in the 1950s is ineluctably associated with the television show "Death Valley Days," which a motel in Bridgeport, CA, outside Death Valley in the Sierras, supplied DVDs of. One was about "Scotty's Castle," and another about a female prospector called "Claim-Jumpin' Jennie" whose prissy daughter, in finishing school back East and ignorant of the way her mother really lives—swinging an axe and wearing male prospector's clothes—shows up in what is now the ghost town of Rhyolite unannounced: she's going back to Independence to dispute a claim: the reality of all these places we'd visited made the show, even in DVD re-runs, seem like a travelogue for the boys.

"Death Valley Days" was presented by 20-Mule-Team Borax. For the ads, actress Rosemary DeCamp, in too-cliched-to-be-mockable 50s housewife-in-high-heels fashion, showed "the girls" watching the program how the laundry additive 20-Mule-Team Borax made their wash brighter! Borax had other applications, yet still it was cause for meditation that so much human, and mule, endeavor, was invested in ripping from the Earth a product whose only purpose was to make whites whiter and brights brighter.

I had noted a grove of palm trees by the road, up by the gas station: this is the oasis for this part of Death Valley. Across the way is the grander hotel than ours that, we learned, would close for the summer season the next day (too hot), a remnant of 20s building of which Scotty's Castle, that I visit later, is another, when the rising curve of American fortune intersected the falling curve of the difficulty of accessing what once had been more lethal than the untrammeled wilderness, this Death Valley. The palm trees produce Death Valley dates—a somewhat surprising notion. But, I reflected, why not here, if the oases of the North African deserts produce them as well? All the trees are propped up with four two-by-fours that make a schematic skirt at their base. I turn up the road into the grove, and discover a path that goes, in a square, around them. Running between the trees is possible too, in the pale light of early morning: the wooden struts are far enough apart that I don't have to weave around them.

But the grove is small, and I am quickly through them. The whole oasis is green as the result of constant watering: the grass between the date palms isn't tourist grass and so it's scraggly, unlike the grass in front of the pool-fronting rooms of the motel's several buildings. Next door is the golf course, lowest in the Americas. You wouldn't know it's low: it just seems hot—only just now, not too hot—and dry—only here, in the irrigated oasis, not too dry. It seems an ideal place to run: here the grass is smooth, there are graveled paths, and the sprinklers go chit-chit-chit.

This is also the only place where anybody's up. The tourists—largely German and Italian, I'd noted yesterday around the pool while the children splashed, though there was a young French family with a new baby—are still asleep, as is my own family. And the highway is deserted. But here in the parking lot of the golf course there are already several cars, and middle-aged men with youthful faces, their bellies expanded under polo shirts, are clustered behind the clubhouse. I run by and wave: one of them looks astonished.

In short order I find out why. I'm a half a mile down curving gravel paths through the perfectly hillocked grass, and I hear a golf cart coming down beside me. It slows, I stop, and a good-natured man at the wheel explains to me that jogging is forbidden. I say I didn't know, saw no sign—he tells me there is one off the parking lot, I say I came from the palm grove. He's not trying to argue, just to do the bidding of the golf players. It's dangerous he says, flying golf balls. I forgo saying the men aren't anywhere near this pat of the course but back down; he's non-threatening but firm, points the way he wants me to run back to the parking lot, not the way I came. I wave and do so, my feet squishing a bit on the grass on water that makes the greenery here in Death Valley. In a bit I am back at the road, running through the parking lot where in fact there is a sign that lists forbidden actions, including jogging.

I feel the weight of my body here in the hovering heat, that I can sense massing around me. The sun is barely up, the air isn't hot, but perhaps it's knowing I'm in Death Valley that dogs my footsteps. On the other side of the road it's desert, and the sun lights up the looming formations on the other rock wall that makes such a dramatic descent from Beatty, NV—the entrance the tourists from Vegas take, and the tour operators, later in the day. At first it's still Nevada, and the land is flat, driving at the looming mountains ahead. Then there is a line on the road, and it's California, and soon the road begins to snake to penetrate the rock wall. And then down: it feels like entering the center of the Earth: only the rock walls around the road are visible, and far ahead, the mountains on the other side of the valley. The rocks acquire strange colors, reds and yellows, what seem green and blue, and the road curves and curves as if wiggling its way into the core of things. And then suddenly the road breaks free of the mountains and below the descent continues into the cup of the valley, stretching for miles ahead before washing back up on the other side: and still the road goes down, and down again.

It's not until my second visit to Death Valley I'm aware of this down, down, down, however: for the first weekend, when I go running, we had taken the back road in, going over the Gilbert Pass and down various unpaved valley roads through the Eureka Valley and by the dunes. We then snaked around some of the most tortuous mountain landscape—the roads rocky and unpaved, the drop-offs vertiginous—that I've ever experienced: only telling myself it wasn't worse than the descent down to Bujumbura on Lake Tanganyika in Africa (it was) helped me keep my nerve. When, later, I drove the almost-straight and paved roads that lead from Beatty, Nevada, and then out at Scotty's Castle, Death Valley lost some of its sense of the remote and harrowing, becoming an easy jaunt from a town rather than a death-defying ordeal through a dusty nowhere.

But here, running along the highway, having been thrown out of the civilized, irrigated preserve of the golf course, where men in polo shirts send the employee in the golf cart to shoo away interlopers, the contrast between our life-threatening entrance and the strange mundanity of this world below is paramount. Even jogging seems put in question here: of course I could take off running down the highway; it seems unlikely I'd meet anyone at this hour of the morning. But how far could I get before the elements claimed me? How far from the date palms of this irrigated oasis? Far enough into the desert to turn around and come back, saying I'd done it, along the endless ribbon of road through this immense valley (driving south from the astonishing black volcano crater of Ubehebe, I'd think we were almost there, and we'd come to a crossroads that said we had another 40 miles to our destination): it seemed senseless, mocking the immensity of where we were.

Or perhaps I was more affected by being thrown off the golf course than I wanted to admit, the near humiliation of these pudgy-faced men who had stared incredulously at the muscular half-naked man—me—putting out more effort in an hour than they would put out in a week, and summoned the groundskeeper to have him evicted. I went once more through the palm trees, aiming now for the swimming pool, where I thought I'd simply swim for twenty minutes.

This turned out to be equally problematic. The Hispanic man sweeping the concrete around the pool informed me that the pool didn't open until 7. He had his work to do. I smiled, spoke to him in Spanish, assured him I didn't want to bother. He looked friendlier, considered, then announced he would call the main office to say I was swimming and he was sure it would be all right. *Esta seguro?* I asked? *Si si*, he reassured me. He disappeared, I waited, he came back smiling: *esta bien*, I could swim.

Here too my wings had been clipped: the freedom of the early-morning-runner, or in this case swimmer, going out before others were up, or doing his laps before the sides of the pool filled with out-of-shape Europeans burning their skin in their ridiculous colored bikinis (and that for the men). I had been given permission here, as I had not on the golf course, but in both cases it was clear that I had to stay within the bounds of civilization. And whyever not, here in Death Valley where the so-artificial civilization was also apparently so-regulated, and the wild valley awaited with its dessication and its coyotes outside of this oasis? Here there was none of the gradual transition of the world I was used to, where leaving the knots of civilization wasn't to flirt with great natural forces, and where even civilization had fewer rules than this seemed to.

Rwanda
Death Valley showed me that running only made sense where the wild wasn't completely wild, and where civilization wasn't guarded so jealously. I should have learned this from my two years in Rwanda. I lived in a fenced-in world of modest third-world houses—my house in Africa was the same construction as university housing I saw later in India, one-story houses with brick outsides, concrete floors that could be sluced clean with water, and bars over the windows, with tin roofs—in the middle of the potato fields here on the extended apron at the base of the volcanoes Karisimbe and Visoke, large and hovering in the sky from a vantage point in my back yard. I ran along the rutted road that left the fenced-in compound of dirt roads and houses, cut rather arbitrarily but no less absolutely from the potato fields that began inches on the other side of the fence, where I had my houseboy put coconut matting so the

women with babies slung onto their backs in colorful wrappers, bent over and hoeing in the volcanic soil, didn't have to look at me sitting in my gazebo listening to the BBC and eating my breakfast of melon, toast, and cheese—or of course, the reverse: it was just too great a contrast.

My run went down to the end of the dirt lane and turned left at the gate to the housing compound in the middle of the fields, which was only a chain-link fence, had no gatepost and was always open. On the right were the low, unprepossessing brick buildings of the university campus that had been inserted here into the fields, five miles down an unpaved road from the nearest village, called Ruhengeri, which was like an African version of a Wild West town: single-story buildings flanking the main road for the proper stores (beer in one, including the local Primus made by a Heineken affiliate) and a great space for the once a week market that came alive on Saturdays with bodies, colors, smells, and foodstuffs. I was soon past the brick classroom buildings and the most impressive building of all, the library and administration building, single-story but large and square and built around a courtyard and without the tin roofs that covered the other structures, individual classrooms connected by tin-roofed walkways. The grass was cut by men swinging machetes, so that every shorn blade was a victory over chaos, the grass a vast mass of 1 + 1 + 1, each plant shortened individually, rather than the whole being the carpet of the West over which a mower passes. The potato cultivation started at the very spot the grass ended, and here things became rockier as well, the volcanic soil producing stones that were picked out of the fields and stacked. Here too were the goat boys, each not with a herd of goats but with a single goat tethered by the side of the road. The women with baskets on their heads walking on the sharp stones with their large naked feet apparently oblivious to what's underfoot turned their whole bodies to see me pass; I greeted them in rudimentary Kinyarwanda and they responded, apparently delighted that such a creature as myself could communicate with them.

I ran by them without a feeling of self-consciousness, as I knew the local villagers were aware that there were white people living at the university as well as rich Rwandans (that is, people who lived in brick houses rather than in huts with dirt floors); they simply accepted my difference from them. They ate to get the energy to work, and here I was running it off to no visible purpose: white people are inscrutable, that's the way it is. At every turn there were more women with baskets, or little boys with goats, or children playing: they looked, or came to see. The only reason not to run would have been to pretend I was playing by their rules, which was obviously impossible. I was different, and all of us knew it: this freed me to do as I liked.

Not so in Death Valley: it seemed like taunting the world to no good effect to simply go running in the desert. Some people feel empowered by challenging nature, rock-climbing without a line, or free-fall parachuting over gorges. Instead of being empowered, these people are diminished. Nature will always win, if provoked, so the game seems to be to come as close to the line as possible without crossing it. It's like feeling powerful by taunting a lion, or touching your hand to the glass that touches the lion's behind. In fact all it does is remind you that if the glass weren't there, you'd be vanquished. It's supposed to be the thrill, this flirting with defeat without achieving it. But since the outcome is guaranteed if you cross the line—like driving too fast to see if you can stay on the road—what's the point? It makes us utterly aware of our servitude, rather than able to look away from it.

Running isn't daring the world, or shouldn't be: it's letting out the line a bit, but still staying within the buffer zone of the permissible so that people don't care. If people do care, people who expect you to be like them, then running becomes a statement, and hence problematic: it's impossible to find the blur, the area where the self disappears into the world, unsullied by interactions with other people.

9
The Abandoned Teddy Bear, or
The Problem Running Solves

Running is a specific action under specific circumstances, in specific times and places, that for the duration of the action adds motion generated from within to the Cartesian duality between mind and body and so unites them both. Running also heals the great modern split between the self and the world, that gulf that is at the center of the Romanticisms of each century from the eighteenth onward.

Running solves the problem of modernity. This is: if the most important thing is my own sensibility, how do I connect with the world outside myself? Running is what connects us. No, the connection isn't in words; it's in action. As posed, the question isn't solvable: that's the nature of big questions. If we postulate a self on one side of a divide and the world on the other, by definition, the two can only be linked by a third entity—and what links that to the other two? The two entities fuse if we simply don't separate them to begin with. Running cuts the Gordian knot, rather than untying it. But that's the way problems are always solved—or at least moved beyond. Perhaps no problem is really ever solved: if it were solvable it wouldn't be a problem, but only a question on the order of, Is that a fly on the wall? Get up and see! Or: do I want vanilla or chocolate? Just choose one!

Renaissances

Most historians of ideas agree that Modernity began in some fashion in the fifteenth century, unless it began in the Renaissances of the ninth or twelfth centuries, or in stronger form in the mid- to late-eighteenth century. Regardless of the date they choose as showing the earliest glimmers of Modernity, what they see dawning is the same in all cases. Namely, a greater emphasis on the value of individual experience, man as the center of all things.

Modernity began with a focus on the human, not the transcendent. The Renaissance of the fourteenth and fifteenth centuries seems the discovery of secularism, the way this world looks, rather than an emphasis on the next—even if this did not necessarily imply the abandonment of religion. Plutarch was famously the first man to have been known to climb a mountain solely to enjoy the view; artists from Donatello to Michelangelo celebrated the beauty of the human body; other painters developed secular portraiture as an alternative to church altars, and gradually landscape emerged as a legitimate subject, starting as a developed side-dish in the paintings of such Flemish painters as Patinir, becoming a genre in the Dutch paintings of the seventeenth century, and achieving primacy in the hands of the Barbizon painters and the French Impressionists in the mid- and late nineteenth centuries. Medicine actually began to look at how bodies worked rather than relying on theories; astronomy placed the Earth and the sun in their proper relationship rather than relying on theology. It was a great acceptance of the temporal, the here and now, the human.

Yet if this is the great achievement of Modernity, it's also the source of Modernity's great disadvantage. The anguish of the Modern is found in the fact that the value of Earthly experience must be found in people, not in apersonal transcendent truths. Thus we find ourselves chained to others, and hence even more aware of our aloneness with respect to them. Of course when the value of life was found in apersonal truths—religions, most typically—this produced its own set of problems. It led to the admirable fervor of the Christian Middle Ages, that form of Faith (whose disappearance Matthew Arnold bemoaned in his poem "Dover Beach") that built the cathedrals, houses of God, high over the roofs of mere human houses, but also led to intolerance of unbelievers such as Jews within the societies and countless wars of religion outside, including the Crusades, based on the perceived need to free Jerusalem from Islam. Within Europe this location of value in the transcendent led to the Inquisition—which made perfect sense in its own terms: surely it's better to lose your mere Earthly life, even as a result of horrible torture, than suffer Eternity as one of the Damned.

The problem with religion is that it's not based on proof. So what do you do with people who deny what you hold dear? Ultimately if they hold out long enough you have to compel them to do as you say. By the Enlightenment, people had lost the taste for this compulsion implicit in religion. And the modern mind has lost to an even greater degree an affinity for this way of thinking: it can still yearn after the transcendent without being able to make what Kierkegaard called the "leap of faith" or indeed finally making it—though either way the notion of the leap shows how daunting and off-putting it really is for a modern, as it would presumably not have been for someone who watched Chartres Cathedral being built.

The nineteenth century was bad enough for Faith, as Matthew Arnold suggested. The twentieth century was worse. The epitaph of the Age of Faith was written not in "Dover Beach" but by Wittgenstein in the *Tractatus*. If it's beyond life it simply can't be said, which really means the converse: if you can talk about it, it's not transcendent. And if it's not transcendent, you can ask whether or not it's true, and demand verification. But the good thing about faith was that it could provide value without verification—the very thing that made religion and metaphysics anathema to the logical positivists who were influenced by Wittgenstein. Still, in pointing out the disadvantage of Faith, they overlooked the advantage: it can provide value for all of life, because it's beyond life. For those who believe, that's the point.

Of course even today we have those who manage the "leap of faith": nuns and priests, Thomas Merton and young people going on a pilgrimage in the footsteps of a martyr. And outside of the secular West the well of faith has clearly not run dry either, at least in the Middle East: Islam is a younger religion than Christianity, and apparently still believes that the transcendent is a matter of collective policy rather than individual conscience, as the modern Westerner believes. This is given legal form in the American separation of church and state, and by the increasing secularism of many Western European countries. Yet the American separation of church and state isn't the death knell of religion; indeed it can be argued that this saved religion for the modern mind, by making it off limits for demands for verification. It's "what I believe," nothing more and so nothing less. By relegating religion to the private sphere, the sphere of recreational running, the American republic gave religion a new lease on life.

Diver's helmet
Yet the problem now is this: if man is the center of all things and we no longer kill for our religion, but regard it as a personal matter, what then creates absolute value in life? If the view is enjoyable because I'm enjoying it, isn't that a bit circular? Is there anything beyond my own sensations? Surely that condemns me to life in a diver's helmet, constantly hearing the sound of my own breathing, aware of the sense of my own sensations. I like what I like because I like it; I perceive what I perceive. If I ask, further, what the point of that is, there's no answer. I enjoyed that, we say. If we say, so?, there's no possible response. Ultimately, every isolated individual will say, so?

The anguish of the early Romantics was realizing that I can't pull myself up by my own bootstraps as far as the world, now so external to myself, is concerned: my perception of or interest in the world cannot be the reason for me being interested in it, and so cannot justify my perception. This in turn led down the cul-de-sac of the Romantic insistence, from Shelley to the Russian Formalists, that the artist somehow rejuvenated, refreshed, or created the world anew: without the artist, therefore, no world, or at least nothing we perceive. It's not enough to perceive the world, you need the artist to give it to you.[21] The artist is the new center of value.

The artists who promulgated this artist-centered view of art, which is to say all the Romantics from Goethe to the twentieth century and even beyond, saw themselves as altruistic: if only people would pay attention to them, they would redeem the world for all the others. Yet of course they were really out for control: control of readers, viewers, listeners. What if all the others didn't want to get their world via art? Many average people, it turned out, wanted their own worlds, not those given them by artists. If you have to go to a gallery to perceive the world, we might as well give up now.

This fact produced the end of art as a collective enterprise: now it was Us vs. Them. If They need Us, the very least they could do is thank us. What artists had failed to realize is that They aren't necessarily going to fall in line to We

(artists) make the world for them, and They (the dreaded bourgeois of
Baudelaire, the Philistines of the English aesthetes) don't even thank us, or
indeed acknowledge our heroic labors. Worst of all, they ignore our works. So
the artists continued remaking the world on their own, even without people
looking at what they'd done, to increasing irrelevance, and increasing anguish.

The problem remained: in the absence of religious belief, a collectively
shared story of meaning, what gives life its purpose? Surely not merely the fact
that we as individuals live it? That's the problem that transcendence, solved,
after all.

So what's next as a source of value? The answer of the twentieth and now
twentieth-centuries was given in embryo in David Riesman's famous theory of
the "other-directed" generation in *The Lonely Crowd*.[22] Instead of being "inner-
directed," like the Victorians (think British colonials faithfully putting on their
white ducks in their jungle settlements and reading each issue of the *Times*
exactly five weeks to the day after it came out, taking only one at a time for
breakfast from a pile that arrived every month with the paqueboat), with our
inside gyroscope, we look to others to give us value. Riesman saw this by the
1950s, and by the end of the twentieth century others as a source of value had
produced the cult of celebrity: people and things are interesting to me because
they are interesting to others. I have to have this X because it's the fashion; a
restaurant is "hot" because others are going to it—so I must too.

The advantage of this source of value is that it transcends most individuals:
if I get value by doing what movie stars are doing, that means that everybody
but movie stars gets value. The disadvantage for the movie stars is usually some
form of "what about me?" poor little rich boy angst. The famous are rarely well-
adjusted, and no wonder: basing value on celebrities works for all but the
celebrities. Whom are they supposed to get value from? Heavy lies the head that
wears the crown of celebrity.

Still, using celebrities as a source of value works for all others. This is by
definition a solution that presupposes mass movements and the reproducible
objects of consumer society. Everybody wants the same Gucci bag, the same
Rolex watch, the same X whatever. Only knockoffs have any reflected value,
because it allows people to pretend they have the Gucci or the Rolex. Something
that's another thing entirely has no value. And what they do has to be amenable
to wide distribution, even if their price is high. Sports and movie figures get
such ridiculous salaries because of the millions of little people each paying their
mite to see them: something like chamber music, with more limited audiences,
has nothing like this star appeal.

Individualists for decades therefore denounced consumer society, from
Walter Benjamin's denunciation of the "aura"-less reproducible work to the
Frankfurt School hatred of non-elite arts, to contemporary Marxists such as
Christopher Lasch, denouncing the intrinsic narcissism of goods-driven value.[23]
Their point is this: if your source of value is other people, you condemn yourself
inexorably to servitude to the masses. In the 1980s some intellectuals realized

that they could adopt another stance with respect to consumer society. They moved from Adorno's defense of the abstruse music of Arnold Schoenberg to the Barbie and Princess Di focus of the "cultural studies" movement.[24] Yet writing intellectual defenses of the masses didn't make those writing a part of these masses. Whether intellectuals were writing for or against mass society, they wanted to be the ones to critique it—not just live it. Their fundamental attempt is still to control the larger society by pinning it to the wall. Whether they love it or hate it, write about Las Vegas and Disney World admiringly or disparagingly, they're still analyzing it, not just going to the rides or the tables. They're still outsiders to what they write about.

We see this sense of outsidership in Paul Fussell's hilarious book *Class*, which heaps scorn on people driven to wear what the author, citing Alison Lurie, calls "legible clothing" (clothes that double as advertisements for their brand); this is the middle classes.[25] Yet the worst class is what Fussell calls "upwardly-mobile proles," people who think it's "classy" to call famous people Mr. and Miss—as in "here she is, ladies and gentlemen, Miss Elizabeth Táylor!" It's all about aping your betters—hardly a new observation, but keyed to America rather than Victorian Britain. And according to Fussell, the only class that escapes the relentless push to ape their betters are intellectuals, who tend to live in colleges. This non-class, the group of all people not trying to pull themselves up but merely do their own thing, are content with their baggy tweeds that last forever, their shabby but interesting houses, which they don't keep up because they're off to dig up something in Turkey or visit someone in Romania with never a thought to what they're "supposed" to be wearing, doing, thinking, or eating. They and they alone are the only free people. They alone are not engaged in seeking value from others.

The conclusion, coming from a professor, is a bit too self-serving to be convincing; still, it's a small contribution to the search for value in the twentieth century. If you merely enjoy things because you enjoy things, it seems you find value without being in servitude to others. You don't have to find out where the Beautiful People are going on vacation; you go to Turkey to your dig, and that's that. You don't have to ask if hemlines are long or short; you just wear your old tweeds. For Fussell, intellectuals are the new Old Rich, not having to keep up with fashion because they use the family silver and the inherited furniture and never going up to town at all. Professors are P.G. Wodehouse's Lord Emsworth, pottering about his pig—or their pots in Turkey.

And indeed, people who are likely to read something like this book are conversant with its realization that you have to get your pleasures where you can, appreciate what you're given: the sunset in your backyard may be fully as spectacular as a sunset in Borneo, where you're "supposed" to go to enjoy it, and you don't have to suffer jetlag to see it. The glass of wine may taste just fine on your back porch; you don't have to go out to a "hot" restaurant to drink it, hoping to see celebrities and basking in the satisfaction of having gotten a table. It may be more interesting, as Virginia Woolf—one of the first of the do-it-yourself value people—suggested in her story-essay "The Mark on the Wall," to watch a moth on the wall than go into dinner with the Prime Minister in the correct Order of Precedence laid down by men of action—men, first, and people of action rather than contemplation.[26] A good book and a plate of leftovers at home might well be more satisfying than sitting through a $1,000 a plate dinner with a celebrity.

The point of these intellectuals is that there's a lot of the world that gets ignored if a million people are all doing the same thing, going to the same place, watching the same movie. Why not enjoy those other things? Besides, many things cannot by definition be enjoyed in public or in a crowd, or with the gaze of others upon it: books, say, or paintings. Their value is not related to the fact that others are looking at them: indeed their value for us diminishes to the extent that others are crowded around them.

If we realize we're not condemned to do what others do what shocks us is the almost wasteful abundance of the world, rather than our inability to get tables for a "hot" restaurant of the fact that we have to save to buy a Rolex. The world is all around us; we need only reach out and take it.

I was stopped today on a shabby road out of Washington, D.C. There was construction ahead. I could fume (I was losing time on my way home from what is called the "monumental core" of Washington), or I could settle back and pay attention to things I was usually, when on this road without construction, moving too fast to appreciate. So I decided to give in and appreciate.

Over on the left was something the steel gray of the late autumn sky turned to a walk-in sculpture: stadium lights one block over, towering over the backs of ramshackle houses, themselves all fire exits and back porches, and in front of them the interestingly corrugated and ripped metal awning of a run-down used car lot, something that belonged more in the Kampala, Uganda of 1986 when I visited, shortly after its civil war, than in Washington D.C. of 2009. And when the traffic finally inched up to the traffic light (two lanes were closed) I got to watch the curdled gray cement trickling down the chute the workers pushed back and forth over the long slit opened in the road so deep I could not see the cement fall.

That was fully as interesting as anything I'd have seen in the contemporary art museum—which is why I rarely go in these any more. Instead, that day, I'd looked at seventeenth century Persian paintings used for divination, something different from the fascinating world of the street so much contemporary art insists—futilely, as it happens, since it's more interesting on the street than anywhere else—on translating to the museum. Such artists are still lost in the Romantic delusion that people need or even expect artists to give them the world, that the place we go to perceive the world is the art museum. Why go to a museum when we can just look out our car window? Or for that matter go for a walk? It's true that people seeking value from other people apparently don't do much perceiving of the world at all, so that books must be written to encourage parents to get their children out into the woods (*Last Child in the Woods*) or to have unstructured playtime.[27] But they certainly don't go to the museum to get that perception. So most contemporary art is useless.

Melancholy

Intellectuals aren't the only ones who see the disadvantage of this way of wringing meaning from the world by doing what others do. The dark side of this attempt to base value on the fact of someone's valuing is melancholy, when we realize just how transitory and unpredictable that valuing is. Melancholy is possible with ourselves: when we realize that what we wanted last year isn't what we want this year. But with ourselves, we still have the this year's desire to tide us over. Most melancholy is sensed with others, specifically with the abandoned objects that once powered desire, and now do so no more.

Ghost towns are one place where even non-intellectuals and college professors sense this melancholy. The West is full of ghost towns. Rhyolite is one of the more celebrated of them, perhaps because it's at what for most people is the entrance to Death Valley, and within two hours of Las Vegas. The visitor to Rhyolite turns off the road running from Beatty to Death Valley and turns up what used to be Main Street, now devoid of intact structures except, at the very end, a Victorian train station surrounded by a fence. To be sure, on the immediate right at the entrance is the celebrated "bottle house," restored to something like its original state, whose walls are the thickness of the colored glass bottles, largely green, of which it's composed: they're held together from rolling off by opaque cement or brick mortar that leaves their ends exposed. According to the informative woman in the Beatty Museum, this was in a sorry state of repair before it was re-done for a documentary movie.

Many people seem to do documentary movies in this area. At the Baja Mexican café in Beatty, we met a camera crew from a PBS station in St. Louis, come to do a show on the Belgian artist whose studio is next to the end of Rhyolite's Main Street (the visitor also passes this on the way in). He makes smaller versions of what look like a cross between Saint-Gaudens's Clover Adams memorial, a body largely obscured by a cloth, and Martha Graham's celebrated sitting sheath dance "Lamentation," where the dancer's face, hands, and feet are all that protrude from a stretchable tube—all in a version of George Segal's chalky whiteness. The sculptures are half-human-sized, ghost-like (the reference to the phrase we use for the town is a bit too obvious not to produce a wince) shrouds for pygmies, probably made by applying plaster-soaked cloth to the outside of a large doll that has then been removed, then these arranged in groups like the shells of miniature Druids gathering for a ritual.

Past the bottle house, however—surrounded by chain link fencing that encloses trash that tourists have thrown here—is a road on the sides of which the viewer sees foundations and sharp fragments of walls from a number of structures. The most evocative is the bank, largely because there is perhaps 2/3 of a wall on the bottom floor still standing—the largest chunk of a building outside the train station. Otherwise the town consists only of what we might call building shards, as if they had been a double row of pots shaken to death by an earthquake. Indeed, it seems only an earthquake that could have wrought such devastation to what, if only for a few years in the early part of the twentieth century, was a flourishing town. Or rather, annihilation, as in causing not to have been: it goes way beyond devastation, and the toppled walls that an earthquake would have left are nowhere to be seen.

It's only possible to imagine the whole pot, or building, because the local historical society has helpfully placed almost surreal photographs of the building once on this site in front of the shards. In the photo before the bank, we see a parade in Rhyolite in the early years of the century, at the height of the town's prosperity, well-dressed people passing in front of what we realize is the bank, whose ruined façade we're looking at. This is the most melancholy of the photographs—others show the street, or a building that isn't visibly connected to the ruins that remain—because we can actually see this part of the wall in the photograph. *Sic transit gloria mundi*, how the mighty are fallen, and so on. The melancholy is in comparing the two states as extremes: on one side, an image or evocation of the town in the full flower of its wealth; on the other side, the shattered remains. What happened in the middle? The melancholy comes from not knowing.

Easterners invented the concept of the "ghost town," which for this part of the world is simply the traces of the passage of humans on their quest for a natural element they can mine and sell—in Rhyolite, it was silver. For Easterners, these abandoned traces of recent habitation take some getting used to, as the abandoned mine shafts that dot Death Valley take some getting used to. Easterners don't think people can simply walk away from habitations or machinery. Here in the West, they can: ghost towns are like trash, left where it falls.

Only most of Rhyolite wasn't left behind at all. When I asked the woman in the Beatty Museum (a single low building with an add-on that looked like a Quonset hut but probably wasn't) why Rhyolite was so ravaged, she informed me that "they loaded it up and carted it away."

"For what?" I asked.

"Building materials," she said.

So they'd destroyed the houses, seen not as solid structures wedded to the land, but rather as agglomerations of components that could be un-agglomerated, carted away like ants carrying grains of sand, and re-built into another anthill. This was a sort of modular town, its parts brought in by the side of a silver mine that, when played out, could be taken away the way nomads set up and strike their yurts in Central Asia. If we understand this, it seems odd to look for ghosts.

Still, we do call places like this "ghost towns." We meander through them, poke through them: we don't run through them. At most, someone staying nearby (but there should be no "nearby" for a ghost town: we don't think of the Roman forum in the middle of a bustling modern city as a ghost town) could run around it, and then down the main street, as I went running around, into, and through the re-peopled ghost town of 18th century Williamsburg. You can run in the modern world in which this fragment is set, treating the buildings as interlopers—but not as an imaginary citizen of the town: they wouldn't have run. You have to be a townsman not of the stiller town, but of your own, the real one that has this place imbedded within it.

Bad man from Bodie

The most celebrated ghost town in the West is Bodie, California. At first glance, Bodie seems like what the doctor of melancholy ordered, like playing the game Keats is apparently playing in his "Ode on Melancholy"—what's the best way to glut a melancholy fit? (Keats's answer is to contemplate a perfect rose or a beautiful woman, because now all they can do is decline from perfection.) Rhyolite seems to fall short; Palmetto (just a few stone walls on a hillside) and the other Nevada ruins just don't make an impression: what about Bodie?

Bodie has a more colorful past, and it even posthumously enters the Mule Days parade in Bishop, which features, what else, mules (as in 20-Mule-Team Borax, as well as pack trains in the mountains, and prospectors' mules). Bodie's entry was a float with bordello can-can girls and masked robbers; the stagecoach-like main vehicle had a banner about the "bad man from Bodie," a concept that survived the town itself. Apparently Bodie bad was worse than the average bad. Or perhaps all this means is that there was too much money floating around in this town up in the hills, for as long as there was money.

Getting to Bodie requires a hard drive up, much of it over rutted and unpaved gravel around twisting curves. Finally there's a Forest Service kiosk, and the friendly ranger takes your money. The town is spread out in fragments in front of you: it's all brown, and looks like a burned forest in which one tree out of twenty is still standing as a crisped ruin. You take the road to the left around the buildings and loop around the town, dotted in the depression before you. By the car park you mingle with the dozens of other tourists who have also followed this twisting road to what was once Bodie. Many are German. Probably they have grown up with the fantasy Western novels of Karl May and are looking for The West.

The space occupied by Bodie is large, though (one is told) only 5% of the buildings survive. The remains of Bodie are held in what is called a "state of arrested decay," which means they're prevented from actually falling down but not otherwise kept up. The church sits open to the elements, with a dirty white fence gate across the empty doorway; inside are pews and walls from which the paint is peeling. The lack of people in the houses means you can peer in the windows: inside it looks as if the people have moved out in a hurry. There's some furniture, largely bedstands, some falling-apart furniture, and scattered magazines. There's almost no paint on any of the buildings, and puzzlingly, each sits next to several vacant lots, or rather empty space not even delineated as much as into lots.

Most of the plots are simply empty: not with building shards, as at Rhyolite, but simply empty earth. The most intact street is Main Street, that leads to the entrance kiosk, though one is only aware of this from Main Street, not from the entrance kiosk: it continues the entrance from the road—when Bodie was Bodie rather than a ghost town, you logically continued down Main Street. Standing on Main Street in Bodie looking out towards the entrance kiosk that diverts traffic is like looking out towards West Berlin from the end of the street by the Glienicke Brücke in Potsdam: you're standing in houses that are invisible from the West, on the other side of the bridge; traffic doesn't just go over the bridge, it has to go out of West Berlin on the other side and come up into Potsdam in a giant loop.

On Main Street, within sight of the entrance kiosk, is the General Store, the hotel, the garage, and the Grange Hall, all of them brown. In the Grange Hall are some objects dug up, many books for sale, and some sense of the industry that is the ghost town of Bodie, with its pre-packaged melancholy. There's an annual Bodie calendar, with evocative pictures of things like the numbers for the hymns still slid in their slots in the church, and a 1930s truck askew and with its front open out behind a building. There are many books; there are souvenirs.

And also some clarity on the nature of the place. Why so many buildings missing? There was a fire, it seems, that wiped out a great deal of the town; the signs of this have been removed. The mine failed, twice. Each time the town lost people. When they went, they loaded up their wagons with movables, which back then didn't include bedstands. So that's why there are so many iron bed frames in Bodie. The houses themselves were valueless, not being made of stones, as at Rhyolite, and in a place where no one wanted to come. So they were simply abandoned: the notion that one sells a house rather than abandoning it is an Eastern idea too, it seems.

The town is not, despite what the promotional material says, "frozen in time." Not even Pompeii, the most celebrated ghost town of all, is "frozen in time": there had been a large earthquake in the year 64 AD, which caused some buildings to fall and people to leave; most others left in the few days of tremors before the big eruption of 79 AD, many taking their belongings. Nor is it like a tumbleweed town where the screen doors flap in the wind. We can see too clearly why it was here, with the great machinery, and understand that the people dealt with the fire, and made the decision to move. We also see what they decided to leave.

Plus it's too pat. The teacher's straw hat in the school window is surely a stage-managed detail, placed within easy view of the window: on the last day of the school (the electricity was cut off to the last hangers-on in Bodie one day in the 1940s) surely she'd have taken her hat, rolled up the map? One suspects some discreet re-arranging of artifacts, perhaps even planting. This is when the visitor begins to feel manipulated.

Less manipulative and thus much more productive of melancholy because not stage-managed and without the Park Rangers or the entrance kiosk are churches I explored down in Somerset County Maryland, their doors creaking to reveal pews covered in pigeon shit, their cabinets disgorging piles of attendance records and donation lists from the 1890s. In Bodie it's not just churches that are abandoned but houses too: plates, broken chairs, magazines, and rats' nests welcome those foolhardy enough to put their heads through the front door. Nobody is asking us to feel anything but aversion down in Somerset County, so we may allow some melancholy to creep in: most people clean up after themselves when they pass on, without these messy trails.

For that matter, why go to Bodie? The world is full of the traces of passage. Every building, every planted tree, every road is the sign of someone's having lived and changed something. It seems in fact odd that we should seek out these "ghost towns" to glut our sense for the melancholy, when the world is full of the transitory that we merely pass over. Perhaps ghost towns are attractive because they're places, part of the horizontal landscape, something we can see and so seems real, rather than being part of the unseen vertical loam that supports us. Plus they're not messy: a museum endowed by someone long gone is as sure a trace of passage as an abandoned *Saturday Evening Post* in a Bodie bedroom, with the bed frame still there, though naked and somewhat askew. But a museum is made of granite and glass, and is full of blue-chip Old Master paintings: no rats' nests, no yellowed paper thrown askew on the ground. So they don't produce melancholy: people have cleaned up after themselves.

Is the source of melancholy, to the extent that we have it in ghost towns, the feeling that the people weren't in control of this world when they left it? This, finally, is the only thing different between a museum (or a house inhabited by many other people, now all long dead) and a ghost town: in a ghost town, we get to see the uncleaned, not-ready-for-prime-time version. Still, in Bodie these were messes people wanted to leave. So in a sense the people who made them were in control as much as those who moved out of a house and cleaned it for re-sale.

In Bodie, we don't think of these people as having lived here, then gone elsewhere to live out their lives, and died off in the natural (or unnatural) order of things one by one. That doesn't inspire melancholy, because it suggests that their absence was a result of their control, and their demise gradual, or at least scattered. For melancholy, we need a sharper contrast; in Rhyolite the melancholy is in the contrast between the photograph of them in high jubilation before a functioning bank, and the building shard, the emptiness. Here today, gone tomorrow: we're aware of the contrast, and so of the jolt. But the jolt is created: if the change was more gradual, we'd cease to react in this way.

Scotty's Castle

The most melancholy spot in the West may in fact not be intended to be melancholy—and end up being the most melancholy for that reason: the contrast between now and then hits us harder when, not waiting for it, suddenly we sense it. This melancholy place isn't a ghost town at all, but a house, what's called "Scotty's Castle," a partially-finished estate perched on the rim of Death Valley.

One of the episodes of *Death Valley Days* in the motel in Bridgeport in the Sierras we'd watched had been on Scotty and Scotty's Castle, punctuated with commercials for Borax that made whiter whites, and the flared skirt of Rosemary De Camp who touted its virtues to the girls. Later, I'd read my guide book. So the outlines of the situation were clear: this was the house of a Chicago insurance executive named Johnson who had met "Scotty," a failed prospector and veteran yarn-spinner, years before in Death Valley and taken a shine to him. Johnson's trip to the desert had cured him of physical ailments doctors had said would kill him young and didn't, all apparently as a result of the hot dry air of Death Valley. Scotty himself was literally a big fat liar, which is to say a fat man and a liar, who claimed to have a gold mine, and who allowed people to think the house built by his patron was his, a fiction into which the patron also entered. Hence the name "Scotty's Castle"—in fact it was "Johnson's Spanish-style Villa," which doesn't have quite the same ring.

Mrs. Johnson was, I'd read, as enamored of Scotty as his patron was: she was half the size of her husband, strait-laced in her own view of religion, tolerating no smoking or drinking and requiring all the household to attend Sunday sermons by herself that lasted for hours. There were no children. And the house, partly built and stalled by the time of the stock market crash of 1929, turned out not even to be on land that Mr. Johnson actually owned: he thought the land he'd bought up in parcels included this piece at the crest of the ridge; later surveying revealed the fact that it didn't—and this after the house was well underway. The small museum with gift shop I saw later had an exhibit that said this had been "resolved," though it wasn't clear how.

Initially I thought "Scotty's Castle" was closed. I was driving up the valley side on a twisting road that led, the sign said, to the "Castle"—the other direction led to the awe-inspiring Ubehebe Crater, coming into Death Valley the adventurous back way at the north end of the valley. I stopped when I saw a gate with a clock in the "Spanish" style I'd seen in the pictures: the architect, I'd read, was the same as for Stanford University's distinctive look. The house, set among palm trees, appeared to be deserted. I pulled into the gate, got out to check, ate a sandwich, and leaned over the wall to look down at the stream, the palm trees, and the greenery within the wall. After a bit I allowed my gaze to wander beyond the stream and the trees, and suddenly I realized I'd stopped too soon: beyond the palm trees was another entrance for cars, the one I was meant to come into: at this hour of the morning, the only other cars had come directly from the main road leading north out of Las Vegas, they hadn't taken the scenic route through the valley that I had.

Several minutes later—after parking, buying a ticket, and waiting—I began to meander until the next mandatory tour. There were a few other tourists about, some sitting in the shade, some circling the house. I had twenty minutes to kill: I killed them by wandering, discovering the unfinished back parts, looking in the windows (most were blocked). And finally it was time to assemble.

By that point it had begun to make a difference whether we were in the sun or in the shade. Everyone sat on a bench by the side of the ticket office, looking at the house. It was a small group. There was a British tour guide from Las Vegas who had seen the house many times before, and sat in the shade for an hour while his charges visited, rather than going in. He had brought several couples, one from Holland, one from Chicago, and two younger men from New Zealand. I know where they came from because the guide, as she stood outside outlining the rules and welcoming everyone (primary rule was "no touching": it was a house, with things sitting out, nothing behind glass). She was a large woman, and a young one. She wore a snood, and high-instep shoes with a short heel that these days are associated with proper British nannies, and a dress made from a print that screamed 1930s. In fact the whole outfit screamed 1930s. I would have been more mystified than I was at this if I hadn't snagged a copy of the *Scotty's Castle Chronicle*, so-called, from the pile in the gift shop. It bore a dateline of 1939, and was a compilation of real newspaper articles from that year (headline was that the truth was out about the true ownership of "Scotty's Castle"—it was actually Mr. Johnson's!) and explanations about the experience one was about to have: the price was an odd amount of money, a specific number of dollars and cents; it turned out tours had been given of the house in 1939 for exactly a tenth of that amount, in dollars not-adjusted-for-inflation. The "Chronicle" also explained that the guides were engaged in "living history" and would be taking us back to 1939.

Our guide observed that we'd surely noted that she was wearing a costume. "Why this costume?" she asked. I already knew, so I watched her gestures, a kind of reach-out-with-the-hand-and-snare-an-invisible-gnat to punctuate the question. She explained that she was part of the "living history" presentation mentioned in the *Chronicle* that, she let drop, had been the condition of the foundation disbursing money for the upkeep of the house. She explained the part she was playing: she was a "wild" niece sent to be straightened out by the famously no-nonsense Mrs. Johnson. She mentioned this story only this once outside in the shade away from the heat, and then again upstairs when we hit the further wing, which turned out to have functioned as a bed and breakfast in the 1930s—so expensive, she told us, that only the like of movie stars could afford it; she herself, at least the role she was playing, had come to help with this. This story told, the rest of the tour, punctuated with the snatching-a-gnat gesture, was identical to the tour a non-relative not in a 1930s snood would have given.

First stop was the garage, an overhanging area onto the courtyard with a large automobile parked by our side as if it had just come in from a ride. The lintel to the house proper, across the courtyard, that we were asked to notice as well gave the real name of the property, not "Scotty's Castle," but "Death Valley Ranch."

I knew that the house was built in the late 1920s, and I probably had come hoping to find some shred of the Jazz Age, a hint of revelries, some wafting music in the Gatsbyesque night. Instead the house was drenched with melancholy in a way that even Bodie was not. There were bowls on the tables as if the people it had once inhabited had just shut the door and gone, yet clearly this was a Rip Van Winkle house, marked by the passage of time. The drip fountain where the fireplace should have been, had long ago broken and had never been repaired, yet if we'd been allowed to touch, we could have sat on the couches. It had been a winter getaway place, so now, in the summer, heavy drapes shrouded the windows.

None of the furnishings—made in California or in Spain, the "niece" informed us; she was a bit vague about their provenance and in any case none was anything more than good, nothing great—merited a label: we were in a house that was somehow halfway between a period room or an "installation" in a contemporary museum and the house of someone famous, where the furnishings matter collectively but not individually. If they hadn't been in Death Valley, they wouldn't be important. Yet it wasn't as if the people who had lived in the house were themselves so important. Or were they? Certainly no one had heard of the Johnsons, except as the owners of this house. And Death Valley Scotty? Only locally famous. Perhaps it was only the unlikely fact of there being a large house like this technically still in Death Valley, even if perched high up on the rim and with no view of the actual valley and no sense of the arid heat of the valley floor?

Off the main sitting room downstairs, the one with the non-working cascade fountain, was "Scotty's bedroom" that, we were told, was only a token and a memorial, not a functioning room—he didn't sleep in this house, though visitors at the time of the Johnsons apparently weren't to know this. The room was scarcely larger than a maid's room, lined with pictures of Scotty's "colorful" past ("colorful" was the adjective constantly being applied to Scotty) as a stunt cowboy, his "trademark" hat and tie (do the same thing over and over and it's a "trademark," apparently), his stories that the entrance to his gold mine was under his bed. On the wall outside his door (there was a door that gave directly to the back of the house, with the unfinished swimming pool, victim of the 1929 crash) was a metal flange between door and window that the guide went to some trouble to explain by enlisting the help of the two New Zeeland men, one stationed as a bad guy at the window and the other about to knock on the outside door: there was a hole in the wall inside the bedroom; this flange was meant to deflect the buckshot from Scotty's shotgun towards both imaginary men, the one postulated to be at the window, the other postulated to be at the door.

Scotty never slept here, and there was no gold mine, certainly not under the bed—as he told all who would listen. So what purpose in objecting to this elaborate story of two thieves (why two?) standing precisely here and here, this strange device that might not even deflect buckshot at all: had it ever been tried? But that wasn't the point. It was all a continuation of the Wild Bill Cody show that Scotty had been in as a younger (and not so tubby) man, of which there were pictures on the walls: a Wild West show peddled to those in search of something that had ceased by then to exist, if ever it had existed at all. That's what he'd sold to them, and they to visitors, and the house, now property of the U.S. Park Service, to us.

Upstairs, student interns were cleaning, one in rubber gloves painstakingly picking up Indian baskets to brush them off, baskets that collected dust all year. The guide said this was the annual cleaning, such as any house might have; it seemed unlikely the maids would have used rubber gloves. She noted we might be able to go into Mr. Johnson's bedroom, otherwise not on the tour. The interns, when asked if we'd bother them, said it was fine by them; we dutifully filed into the bedroom, an ordinary bedroom that could have been in any house, with nothing even "Spanish" about it. Off the bedroom, however, was Mr. Johnson's clothes closet: he'd been dead more than half a century, and his clothes still hung here in rows. Were they too handled with rubber gloves? Surely when a house is put on show the clothes are removed.

But that was the ambiguity of this house: it was trying to be a museum, but had after the childless Mrs. Johnson's death, which followed that of her husband by quite some time, been willed lock, stock, and barrel to a Christian organization, which had kept it as a function hall downstairs but hadn't touched the upstairs, even leaving the clothes in the closets. Or had not touching it been part of the bequest? It seemed creepy. The organization after some years found the upkeep too steep and the house falling apart, and sold it to the government, which runs Death Valley National Park. And here it was, caught uneasily between functioning house and a meant-for-tourists shell, like a half-decayed insect that isn't living insect nor collectable husk, but half-full of soft parts, like as not devoured by the ants. Should be Indian baskets be cleaned, as in a house, or put behind glass, as in a museum? Should the clothes not be removed from the closet? Shouldn't the fountain be made functional? Shouldn't the sun drapes be removed from the windows?

The strangeness of the house came too from the fact that everything here was fake, and had always been so. The piano was a player piano, since neither Johnson was musical; the organ, later used by the religious organization, worked from rolls. The dining room had a set of Spanish dishes, some of which were clearly meant for shelf display only and had a crinkled bottom rim to sit straight on the shelf; next to them sat stacks of the functional ones—an ingenious idea, I thought. Yet the guide explained to us, crowded around the table, that Scotty— who didn't live in this house at all—sat in the large chair given its own niche in the corner and told guests at table tall tales, including the story that one plate had melted on the edge in the intense Death Valley heat. I pointed out that all the plates standing up against the back wall on the shelf were similarly crinkled, and obviously so as merely to be for display and not fall off their perch. The functional pottery, plates with normal edges, sat in piles next to them. The guide wasn't sure what to make of that; perhaps her story merely embroidered Scotty's lies, or she'd got it wrong, or Scotty had decreed that all the flat-edged plates but one be removed, the better to set up his story.

One corner of the dining room was set up like a king's dais, with the armchair under a corner overhang (the only one of the four corners in the room so treated) to make a sort of baldaquin. The idea of a big fat liar sitting in the corner of the room and spinning tales as a sort of dinner entertainment was appalling: the more so in that Mrs. Johnson tolerated neither his drinking nor his smoking (which is why Scotty actually lived five miles away, in a separate house that we could hike to, we learned, with advance notice). It was difficult to imagine: had conversation ceased when Scotty spoke? Were guests to keep respectful silence at table?

Where was the Jazz Age in this unfinished house stopped by the Great Depression and in any case owned by religious bigots who tolerated no merrymaking and took in paying guests to make ends meet? The upstairs bedrooms had been rented out for movie folk—eager then as now, it seemed, to check out "Scotty's Castle," this unlikely villa perched in the green lip of Death Valley. Only one of these rooms was striking, and that because it was large; the others were small and nondescript. This is where the "niece" told us she helped out; here she remembered, if only briefly, to return to her story. She was a sort of maid as well as tour guide. Surely we hadn't come to be caught in an endless loop of seeing ourselves, tourists coming to see the tourists who had come before us?

There was nothing of Gatsby here, no beautiful flitting girls in the night, no longing for the green light on the other shore: only a now-abandoned (the clothes in the closet suggested this, at least) house of a mis-matched couple between whom it was difficult to imagine physical closeness (he was tall, she short: the guide pointed out the abnormally high shower in the bathroom and the abnormally low sink; he was a semi-invalid and she a religious prude), both infatuated in whatever manner with the same sad fake who apparently brought spice to their otherwise drab lives, filled the vast emptiness between them, and had given them a passkey to Death Valley.

Mr. Johnson was quoted in several places in the ticket-kiosk exhibition as saying that "Scotty repaid him in laughs." What must they have thought as they listened for the thousandth time to the story of the melted plate? If it was paying customers who heard it, the Johnsons were relegated to the role of proprietors of a B and B. And now the house sat half as they'd left it, half simply walked-out-of and half gone to seed, the clothes hanging eerily in the closets, the fountain unworkable, the sun fading the drapes more and more with every passing year.

The music room was, to be sure, interesting enough to be the poor second cousin once removed of comparable rooms at, say, Dumbarton Oaks in Georgetown, or the less impressive one in the Hyde Mansion in Glen's Falls, New York: those at any rate had important if relatively fragmentary or minor artworks, and sweep. Scotty's Castle had a player organ that took up the whole side of the room: the guide put a record in it and it duly played "The Stars and

Stripes Forever." Who had listened to this? The paying guests? Not Scotty. Perhaps no one, any more than to the playepiano downstairs.

This was melancholy too deep for tears.

Children

Yet we need not go anywhere to sense this melancholy, not even to the rim of Death Valley—or to understand the problem running solves. We need only pay attention in our own families. The melancholy of objects when human interest is withdrawn from them is the lurking shadow of our quest, being moderns, to find meaning in the attention of others. Some of the love with which we watch children, especially our own, move through the phases of their successive enthusiasms, comes from the fact that we know how transitory and how intense these desires are, and they apparently do not. For them, each enthusiasm is absolute, a be-all and end-all. The short-lived nature of each so-intense interest doesn't seem to be clear to them: they see the world as $1 + 1 + 1 + 1$. This month's pirates suddenly mutate to soldiers; the Indians that waned last month are back with a vengeance. How melancholy.

We sense this melancholy strongest while cleaning out a now-departed child's room—now departed both from childhood and from the house. Suddenly we see the tattered and much-loved objects that we probably remember being the center of their days and interests: here they are abandoned. The object now is the same as the object before, or is startlingly similar: the Teddy Bear pulled from a box bears the same fraying, scuffs, and scars as the day he was abandoned.

What stops us in our tracks is realizing that only the interest of the now-gone child animated this to begin with. This interest might just as well have animated another stuffed animal, or something else entirely, or nothing. Without the child who toted and dragged it about by a single paw, the brown bear whose arm is dislocated from the dragging and that's lost one enamel eye is just trash. At most, someone coming on it in an "antique store" would note the love lavished upon it, and stand for a moment lost in thought before putting it down: nobody wants a scuffed Teddy Bear, least of all another child. There's the object, essentially the same if a bit the worse for wear or the passage of time, yet it has no value whatsoever, not for us, not for anyone. Yet apparently it did, once. Suddenly our path seems strewn with things that we too could not live without, and now have been abandoned: if, in the normal run of thing, we've simply built over them, or thrown them away, we're not required to face this gap between the object and what we added to the object that's now evaporated.

These must be objects of private interest, not collective. Pictures of us in now-unfashionable too-large or too-small eyeglasses such as were fashionable decades ago, too long hair or too wide collars, ties, or shoulders, may cause us to cringe, but they don't induce melancholy. We shrug and grin—that was the 70s, we say. The decade that fashion forgot (as one maven has put it). Or the 80s:

everybody was doing it back then. We may not know what inspired us, but at least the madness was general.

Childhood enthusiasms are particular, not general. We're pleased when we see some use in later life of, say, a collector's mania: the child with the boxes of butterflies on pins becomes a lepidopterist; the child with tanks of fish an ichthyologist. That may make us think the enthusiasm had its point. However, the connection between play and adulthood is rarely so direct; it's not often the child who played with the toy soldiers becomes a career military man. Proud parents may enthuse over Bobby's blatting away on the trumpet on the grounds that he might lead the band; it rarely even comes to this, and more rarely still leads to a professional career.

The purpose of parents is precisely to be interested in the child, whatever he or she is interested in: our function, it seems, is to keep track of the changes of the child, be the people who care. Parents usually save the cast-offs of childhood, at least for a time.

Our lives consist of trajectories through the maze. But it's not the trajectories that are saved, only the thing that drew us on. What to do with the pile of neatly-completed crossword puzzle books we find in a chest? They're used up, ruined. They have to be thrown away, though clearly they meant something to the person who invested all those countless hours in them. Even most collections—leaves, insects—are valueless to anyone but the collector: the countless boxes of broken, dessicated bugs that little boys collect stand as typical. These are simply thrown away when the room is cleaned out.

A pressed leaf fell out of a copy of Booth Tarkington's 20s classic *Penrod* I bought up the road from my mother's Adirondack house, on the banks of the Hudson (there a mid-sized shallow river burbling over rocks), and smelling of old age and mold. On it was written, neatly, in the spidery correct handwriting that not even the old produce any more, "Poplar leaf." Not "Poplar," taking for granted that everyone would understand it was a leaf, but "Poplar leaf." This once meant something to someone, so much that she (to judge by the handwriting) or he (to judge by the book) wanted to categorize it and preserve it. Where had the person lived that poplars merited having their leaves dried? Yet somehow things had stopped there: it had never joined a proper collection, a boy's set of bugs on pins, or frames of leaves. What if there were cases and cases of leaves, all so neatly labeled, and discovered in an attic, or in the back of a garage in the house we had bought and were cleaning out? We'd have stood lost in thought. What to do with them? Their use was only private, a goal, now achieved by a person long dead, or at least long over these goals. A single leaf was less problematic: I could always throw it away. For that reason I could also let it linger on the dashboard of my car, as I ultimately did.

The world is full of things that once meant something to someone. But it's only the cast-offs, or the things we don't want ourselves, that seem melancholy—not the treasures we still value, like the treasure of Tillya Tepe. A great jewel that's passed through many hands. We want it, others wanted it; the object seems to retain its intrinsic value. If we comment on the paradox of the fact that so many people have expended so much (and perhaps died in the process) to possess this piece of pressed carbon, a mineral dug from the Earth, it's in strictly formulaic terms, and it's all been said before—the paradox is too general, we can't add anything.

Another maze

A letter to an advice columnist I read years ago sums up the futility of thinking that the objects at the end of the maze have value in themselves other than through what we add ourselves. A woman writes in, anguished, that she has no children or family members to give her numerous scrap-books to. What should she do with them? The advice columnist, clearly a kind person, suggests the local history society.

Yet this won't solve anything. Even if the local history society wants this woman's scrap-books, it won't be as *her* scrap-books, but as the typical images of a time-period. Without descendents, she ceases to matter. And not even descendents care in the way she'd like them to care. Children who have lived through some of these things can perhaps have a limited interest in seeing how they looked from an other, adult, perspective. Or they're interested in things in their relatives' lives that they weren't a part of because of the fascination with the very notion of the lives of their parents before they themselves entered.

But past a certain point they can't understand the meaning of the object to the deceased parent. My father's silver napkin ring is amidst the clutter of a box in my dresser. I can't place it in context, have no idea what it meant to him. It's just a silver napkin ring. If I discover one day it's only silver plate, it'll perhaps seem a bit tawdry, given that I have no warm feelings for my father to make up for the diminution of absolute value, in any case not large: silver is fairly inexpensive. If I don't tell anyone it was my father's, it becomes meaningless, to be sold for a few dollars in an "antiques" store.

Most of the things we do don't end in anything that will matter to the next generation, or to anyone else. They're used up in the moment, powered only by ourselves, and then we are gone. When they leave these strangely vacant shells, like a Teddy Bear, we feel melancholy. But most of our actions don't even leave shells.

Others' interest in the world, or our own, doesn't give meaning to life. We feel melancholy when it seems to us that something needs to be done with all these interests, feelings, experiences—the stuff that composes most of life—and nothing is being done with them: realizing that most of the things people do don't, in this sense, go anywhere.

Or we can run, which is the alternative to melancholy: running says no, life doesn't go anywhere, which is why I can. I'm moving anyway; I can will myself to move faster and more intensely. I can't be other people, so I will move in response to them, on the edges they leave. I have chosen to do this; in running I merge with the world, my action its own end.

Endnotes

[1]   http://www.bowker.com/index.php/press-releases/563-bowker-reports-us-book-production-declines-3-in-2008-but-qon-demandq-publishing-more-than-doubles.

[2] I consider this performance in *Sex, Art, and Audience: Dance Essays* (New York: Peter Lang, 2000), 196-199.

[3] Ludwig Wittgenstein, *Tractatus Logico-Philosophicus* (New York: Routledge and Keagan Paul, 1963).

[4] Ibid., 6.54.

[5] Martin Heidegger, *Being and Time* (New York: Harper Perennial, 2008).

[6] Virginia Woolf, "The Mark on the Wall," extensively reprinted, and at http://www.readprint.com/work-1523/The-Mark-On-The-Wall-Virginia-Woolf.

[7] Jean-Paul Sartre, *Being and Nothingness* (New York: Washington Square Press, 1976).

[8] Gilbert Ryle, *The Concept of Mind* (New York: Barnes and Noble, 1949).

[9] Alfred North Whitehead, *Process and Reality* (New York: Free Press, 1979), 39.

[10] Michel Foucault, *Madness and Civilization: A History of Insanity in the Age of Reason* (New York: Vintage, 1988).

[11] Jim Fixx's breakthrough book was *The Complete Book of Running* (Collingwood, Vic./Australia: Outback Press, 1977).

[12] Henry LaFarge, ed., *Lost Treasures of Europe: A Pictorial History* (New York: Pantheon, 1946).

I have considered this issue in "Skirting the Precipice: Truth and Audience in Literature," *Antioch Review* 56 (1998): 334-356.

[14] *Aladdin* (film), dir. Ron Clements and John Musker, Disney, 1992.

[15] Woody Allen, "The Kugelmass Episode," *Side Effects* (New York: Ballantine, 1986), 59-78.

[16] Arthur C. Danto, *Encounters and Reflections: art in the historical present* (Berkeley: University of California Press, 1997); *Embodied Meanings: Critical Essays and Aesthetic Meditations* (New York: Farrar, Straus, and Giroux, 1994).

[17] *Citizen Kane* (film), dir. Orson Welles, Mercury Productions, 1941.

[18] *Tractatus*, 5.6331.

[19] Jean Baudrillard, *Simulacra and Simulation (The Body, In Theory: Histories of Cultural Materialism)* (Ann Arbor MI: University of Michigan Press, 1995); *America* (New York: Verso, 1989).

[20] Robert Venturi, *Learning From Las Vegas: The Forgotten Symbolism of Architectural Form* (Cambridge MA: MIT Press, 1976).

[21] I considered this pairing in *Modernism and its Discontents: Philosophical Problems of Twentieth-Century Literary Theory* (New York: Peter Lang, 1992).

[22] David Riesman with Nathan Glazer and Reul Denney, *The Lonely Crowd: A Study of the Changing American Character*, New Haven CT: Yale University Press, 1961.

[23] Walter Benjamin, The *Work of Art in the Time of Mechanical Reproduction*, New York: Classic Books America, 2009; Max Horkheimer and Theodor Adorno, trans. Edmund Jephcott, *The Dialectic of Enlightenment* (Stanford, CA: Stanford University Press, 2002); Christopher Lasch, *The Culture of Narcissism: American Life in an Age of Diminishing Expectations* (New York: Norton, 1991).

[24] As for instance in E. Simon During, ed., *Cultural Studies Reader*, 3rd Ed. (New York: Routledge 2007).
[25] Paul Fussell, *Class: A Guide Through the American Status System* (New York: Touchstone, 1992); Alison Lurie, *The Language of Clothes* (New York: Holt, 2002).
[26] Virginia Woolf, "The Mark on the Wall."
[27] As for example, Richard Louv, *Last Child in the Woods: Saving our Children from Nature-Deficit Disorder* (Chapel Hill, NC: Algonquin Books, 2008).

Index

White Mountains (CA), 80
White, E.B.
   "Once More to the Lake," 20
Whitehead, Alfred North, 8
Wittgenstein, Ludwig, 1, 5, 6, 28, 33,
   90

Wodehouse, P. G., 125
Woolf, Virginia, 7
   "Mark on the Wall, The," 125
wrestling, 72
Xlibris, *iv*
Yosemite National Park, 83

About the Author

Bruce Fleming is the author of numerous books ranging from aesthetics and literary theory (*An Essay in Post-Romantic Literary Theory*; *Modernism and its Discontents: Philosophical Problems of Twentieth-Century Literary Theory*) and more general philosophy (*Art and Argument: What Words Can't Do and What They Can*; *Sexual Ethics*; *Science and the Self*; *The Thanksgiving Symposium*; and *The New Tractatus: Summing Up Everything*), to political and military theory (*Why Liberals and Conservatives Clash*; *Bridging the Military-Civilian Divide*), dance criticism (*Sex, Art, and Audience*), and literary criticism (*Chaos and Order in Modernist Works*; *Caging the Lion: Cross-Cultural Fictions*; *Literary Criticism in a New Key: Homage to Eugene O'Neill*) as well as more general essays (*Disappointment*). He has also published shorter pieces in many quarterlies and magazines, including the *Yale Review*, *Virginia Quarterly Review*, *Antioch Review*, *Southwest Review*, the *Washington Post*, *The Nation*, the *Village Voice*, and the *Chronicle of Higher Education* as well as scholarly venues. He has won an O. Henry short story award; his novel *Twilley* was compared by critics to works by Henry James, T.S. Eliot, Proust, Thoreau, and David Lynch. In 2005 he won the Antioch Review Award for Distinguished Prose, a career award.

Bruce Fleming is a graduate of Haverford College with subsequent degrees from the University of Chicago and Vanderbilt University. He was a Fulbright Fellow at the Free University Berlin and has studied in Paris and Siena. He has taught for more than two decades at the U.S. Naval Academy in Annapolis, Maryland, the subject of his memoir *Annapolis Autumn*. Before coming to Annapolis, he taught for two years each at the University of Freiburg and, as the Fulbright Professor, at the National University of Rwanda. He lives in Maryland with his wife and children.